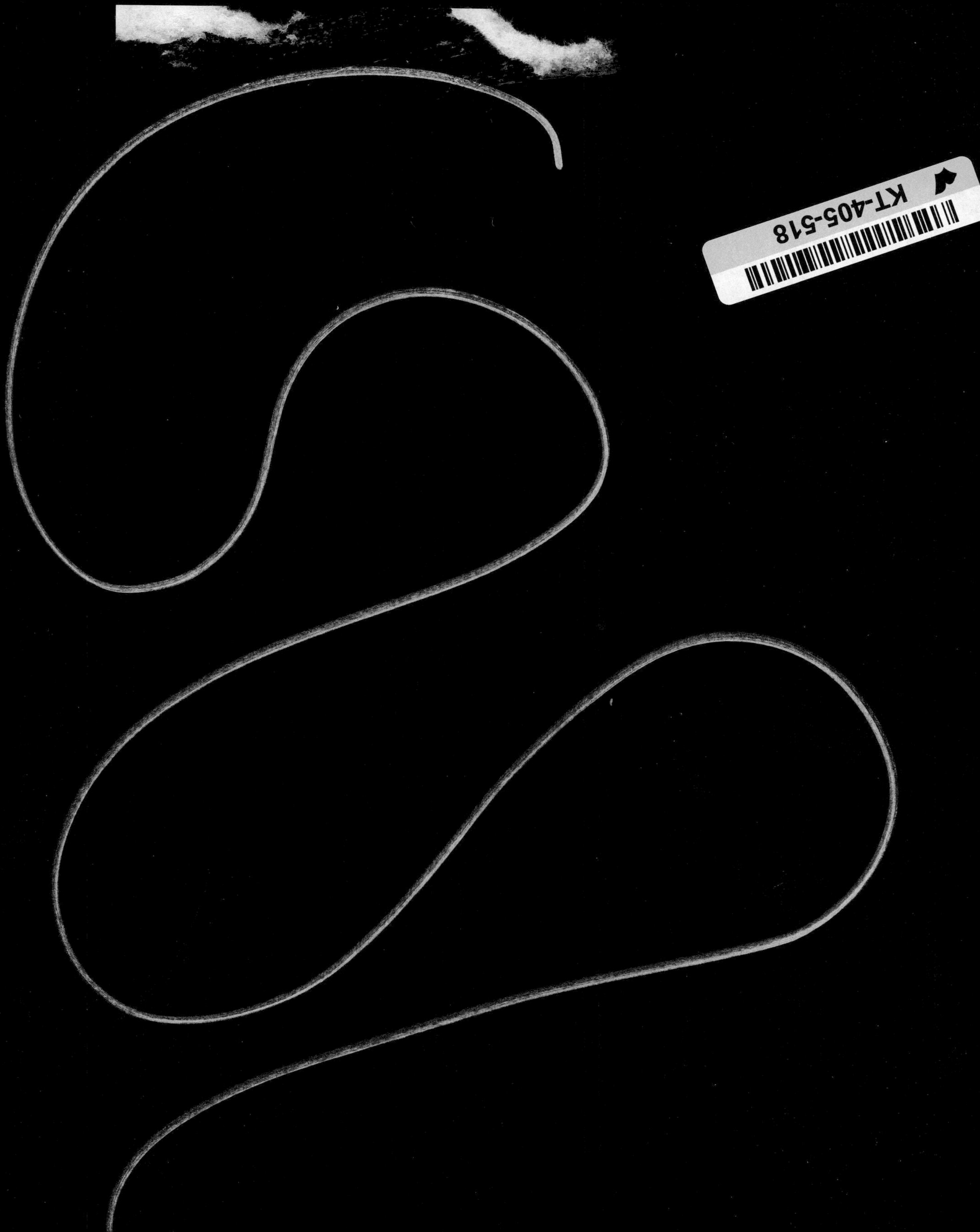

Wembley Stadium
Venue of Legends

Prestel Verlag
Königinstrasse 9
80539 Munich
Tel. +49 (0) 89 24 29 08-300
Fax +49 (0) 89 24 29 08-335

Prestel Publishing Ltd
4 Bloomsbury Place
London WC1A 2QA
Tel +44 (0)20 7323-5004
Fax +44 (0)20 7636-8004

Prestel Publishing
900 Broadway, Suite 603
New York, N.Y. 10003
Tel +1 (212) 995-2720
Fax +1 (212) 995-2733

www.prestel.com

Prestel books are available worldwide. Please contact your nearest bookseller or one of the above addresses for information concerning your local distributor.

Library of Congress Control Number: 2007929940

British Library Cataloguing-in-Publication Data: a catalogue record for this book is available from the British Library. The Deutsche Bibliothek holds a record of this publication in the Deutsche Nationalbibliografie; detailed bibliographical data can be found under: http://dnb.ddb.de

Design and layout by Small, London
www.studiosmall.com
Produced by Firmengruppe APPL
Printed on acid-free paper

ISBN 978-3-7913-3773-9

WEMBLEY STADIUM

Wembley Stadium
Venue of Legends

PATRICK BARCLAY
KENNETH POWELL

PRESTEL
MUNICH BERLIN LONDON NEW YORK

1923

1924

1930

1948

1953

5

1966

1977

1985

FEED THE WORLD
HE WORLD
WEMBLEY STADIUM
LIVE
AID
DIAMOND
VISION

1996

2000

OODBYE
TWIN
OWERS

2007

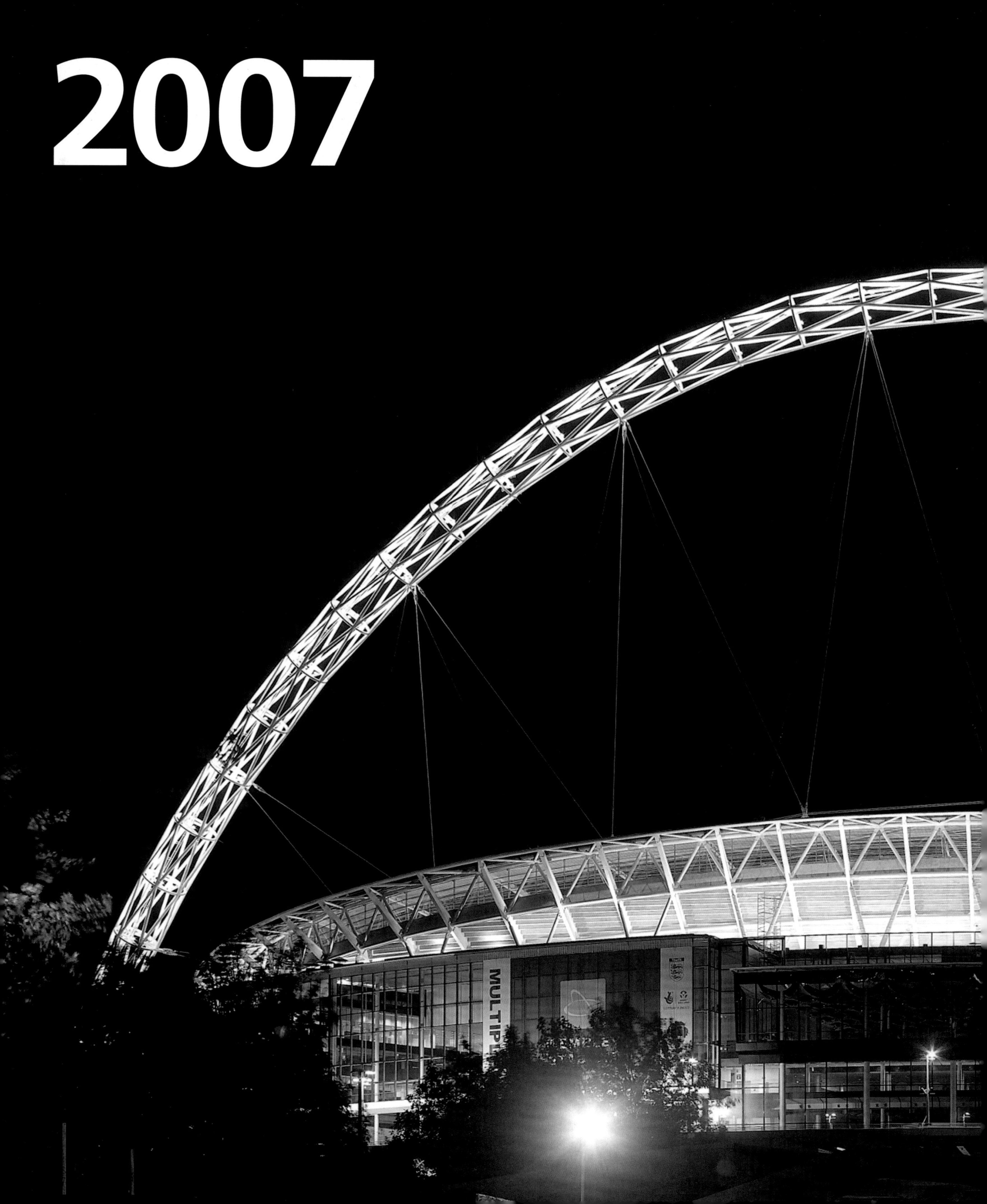

WEMBLEY
STADIUM
MULTIPLEX

Contents

Opposite — The heavy leather ball awaits an FA Cup Final kick-off between Everton and Sheffield Wednesday at Wembley Stadium, 14 May 1966.

THE ROAD TO WEMBLEY

Kenneth Powell

Wembley Stadium is hallowed ground for football fans – the ultimate destination in the 'beautiful game'. The new stadium is the most advanced and best equipped in the world. However, it is also rooted in tradition, drawing on 80 years of history at Wembley to combine the spirit of the old with the best of the new.

The old stadium was established on the world map by the Empire Exhibition of 1924 and the Olympic Games of 1948 – great events in their time that have now largely faded from memory. It also hosted a wide variety of great sporting and cultural events – including a Papal Mass, the historic Live Aid concert of 13 July 1985 and twelve concerts by the Rolling Stones. But its true fame rested on its role as the venue of the 1966 World Cup Final – an iconic event for English football in every respect.

Seeing the new stadium today, one might be surprised to learn that well into the Victorian period – the era that saw the rise of football as a mass spectator sport – the ground on which it stands was little more than 'broad acres, pleasant pastures watered by many streams, extensive waste and commons, and a hamlet or two isolated from the world at large'. Most of the land belonged to a large country estate, Wembley Park, whose grounds were laid out by the great landscape gardener Humphry Repton. The small village of Wembley was far from the main routes to and from London and the first railway lines into the capital bypassed the area completely. It was only with the coming of the Metropolitan Railway that Wembley began to develop as a suburb, the gateway to 'Metro-land'.

The Metropolitan, which opened in 1863, was the world's first underground railway. Initially it ran four miles from Paddington to Farringdon, but was later extended to form the route of the Underground's Circle Line, with branches to Whitechapel, Hammersmith and Swiss Cottage. From the mid 1880s on, under the chairmanship of Sir Edward Watkin MP (1819-1901), the Metropolitan embarked on a massive expansion programme, with a new main line extending into rural Buckinghamshire and turning Rickmansworth, Chesham, Amersham and even distant Aylesbury, which was reached by the railway in 1892, into potential commuter settlements.

Watkin was a visionary, but most of his visions ended unhappily. He was the first, for example, to imagine a Channel Tunnel linking England and France, though his tunnel got no further than trial boring. But perhaps the most spectacular of his failed visions was his attempt to bring a touch of Paris to London with the development of Wembley Park, which the Metropolitan acquired for £32,500 in 1890. Wembley Park station opened in October 1893. On one level, the project was a success, since during the inter-war years part of the area was developed as a residential suburb, 'its picturesque layout ... further advanced by the skilful blending of the varying types of houses'. However, Watkin's bid to turn Wembley Park into a massive sports and leisure centre for London was, at best, premature.

The centrepiece of Watkin's masterplan for Wembley – appropriately for someone who proposed to link Manchester to Paris by rail – was a London version of the Eiffel Tower. Gustave Eiffel's spectacular tower was constructed for the Paris Exposition Universelle of 1889 and quickly became a popular symbol of the French capital. Prompted by the Eiffel Tower's huge commercial success, Watkin and a group of fellow enthusiasts launched a competition in November 1889 for a 'Great Tower in London', the site yet to be decided.

Eiffel was asked to produce designs but declined on the grounds that for a Frenchman to accept the commission would be unpatriotic. Sir Benjamin Baker, the designer of the Forth Bridge, was subsequently recruited as consulting engineer and chairman of the competition jury. The only fixed requirement of the competition brief was that the London tower should be at least 46 metres taller than the 300-metre tower in Paris. Amongst the 68 ambitious and bizarre schemes submitted were an 'upright Tower of Pisa' constructed of granite, a cathedral tower made of iron and steel, a glazed funnel containing 12 pneumatic lifts, a giant corkscrew, and a tower to be inhabited solely by vegetarians, complete with hanging gardens. The *Builder* magazine described them as 'as curious a collection of objects as it has been our bad fortune to see in many a day'.

The winning entry bore a marked resemblance to Eiffel's prototype, though it carried lavish 'Oriental' or 'Indian' detailing. It was to be 350 metres tall and the cost was estimated at £352,222 – a colossal sum. A series of platforms extending up the tower would house restaurants, theatres, a dance hall and a Turkish bath. Work began on the structure during 1893 and by early 1895 it had been constructed to first platform level, 47 metres above the ground. It rose no higher.

The far from spectacular views over Neasden and Harrow failed to excite the London public and the expected crowds never materialised. The structure itself – 'Watkin's Folly' – began to subside into the Wembley marshland and was eventually closed in 1907. Even its demolition with the aid of dynamite attracted only a small crowd of onlookers.

After the failure of the tower, much of the land at Wembley Park was slowly developed for housing – no more than 100 houses had been built by 1914 – with part becoming a golf course for a time. The site of the tower itself remained undeveloped into the years after the First World War. In 1921 it was named as the site of the British Empire Exhibition and early the following year most of the remaining land at Wembley Park was sold to the British Empire Exhibition Assets Company Ltd for £67,323.

The idea of such an exhibition extended back many years, but the contribution of the Dominions and Colonies to victory in the war strengthened the case for its final realisation. The main objective of the exhibition was to foster trade between the countries of the Empire – 'it is only by a general revival of trade that we may hope to reduce the amount of unemployment in this country and bring happiness and prosperity to the homes of thousands of our countrymen who have been passing through a long-drawn period of depression and distress', the Prince of Wales (later King Edward VIII) commented. On 10 January 1922, the Prince, as president of the exhibition, ceremonially dug the first turf.

The 1924 Exhibition, 'a family party, to which every part of the Empire is invited', was to be open for little more than six months that year (from April to November) and all the structures associated with it were to be temporary. Each of the countries of the Empire was to have its own pavilion, its size and style reflecting the importance and something of the culture of the territory in question. In addition, there were to be four pavilions representing Britain's own achievements – the Palaces of Industry, Engineering and Arts, together with a pavilion devoted to the British Government. There was also to be a stadium accommodating up to 125,000 spectators, this alone to be a permanent structure within the grounds. The architect for the buildings and the masterplanner of the site was Maxwell Ayrton, partner of Sir John Simpson, a former assistant of the leading architect of the day, Sir Edwin Lutyens.

The layout of the exhibition was Beaux-Arts in inspiration, with clear echoes of Lutyens' work in New Delhi and with the principal buildings (the Pavilions of Industry and Engineering and the Australian and Canadian pavilions) arranged along a processional avenue, Kingsway (later renamed Olympic Way and often referred to affectionately as 'Wembley Way'), which led southwards from Wembley Park station to the stadium. Formal gardens and a lake formed an east-west axis at the centre of the site along which the other buildings were arranged. Given the tight schedule for constructing the buildings, the extensive use of reinforced concrete was a bold and sensible move. All the exhibition buildings, including refreshment kiosks, drinking fountains, seats and other minor structures, were built of concrete.

Simpson & Ayrton had no experience in building in concrete on such a large scale so the young engineer Owen Williams was brought in to work with them. (Williams won a knighthood, at the age of 34, for his work on the exhibition and on the back of it launched a distinguished career that extended into the 1960s.) Internally, the pavilions featured steel and glass roofs in the best tradition of factory design. Externally, they were predominantly Classical, with concrete used to create the effect of solid masonry. The major pavilions were colossal in scale: the Palace of Engineering covered 46 square metres, all on one level, and had a footprint larger than that of the stadium. The Palace of Industry was only slightly smaller.

The national pavilions reflected the multiplicity of cultures within the Empire, Canada, Australia and New Zealand – Canada's featured a sculpture of the Prince of Wales on his horse made of best Canadian butter, Australia's a complete sheep station, New Zealand's an elaborately decorated Maori house. The Indian pavilion was inspired by the Taj Mahal, though inside could be seen drawings and models of Lutyens' work in New Delhi, then under construction. The West African pavilion, representing Nigeria, the Gold Coast and Sierre Leone, took the form of a village of thatched huts exhibiting native crafts, plus 'wooden idols of immense size and unattractive aspect'. The West Indies pavilion had a garden where coffee, cocoa and bananas were planted, though they did not thrive in the boggy soil.

Within the Palace of Industry, there were stands for companies such as Wedgwood, Bird's Custard and Pilkington, while whole sectors such as the Scotch whisky industry, tobacco, cotton, gas and building sponsored an elaborate collection of stands that reflected the eclectic style of British architecture in the 1920s. The highlight of the Palace of Arts was the Queen's Dolls' House, designed by Lutyens and exquisitely fitted out by leading artists and designers of the day – 'the most remarkable achievement of British Art and Craftsmanship that has ever been accomplished', exclaimed the official guide to the exhibition.

Critical reactions to the exhibition varied but few were enthusiastic about the architecture. The public, however, came in droves. During the six months following the formal opening by King George V – on St George's Day, 23 April 1924 – 'Wonderful Wembley' attracted more than 17 million visitors. The success of the exhibition was such that it was decided to reopen it the following year when, despite a dismally wet summer, nearly 10 million people paid for admission.

The poet John Betjeman, who visited Wembley as a young man, recalled that the amusement park, with its giant switchback, scenic railway, dance hall and aquarium, 'the largest and most comprehensive pleasure park known to history', was by far the most entertaining attraction. Even King George and Queen Mary took a trip on the miniature railway and were filmed enjoying the ride. Like the Festival of Britain a quarter of a century later, the Empire Exhibition was 'a tonic for the nation'.

01

02

03

When melancholy Autumn comes to Wembley
And electric trains are lighted after tea,
The poplars near the stadium are trembly
With their tap and tap and whispering to me.

JOHN BETJEMAN, HARROW-ON-THE-HILL

01 The proposed pleasure gardens of Wembley Park circa 1900. Acquired by the Metropolitan Railway in 1890, for £32,500, Wembley Park was intended to bring a little Parisian chic to the new London suburb. A plan for a massive sports and leisure complex in the park never emerged.

02 The picturesque lake at Wembley Park; the unfinished Wembley tower, 'Watkin's Folly', is in the background.

03 Intended to rival the Eiffel Tower in Paris, Watkin's Folly only ever reached first platform level, 47 metres above the ground. It was eventually dynamited to make way for the British Empire Exhibition of 1924.

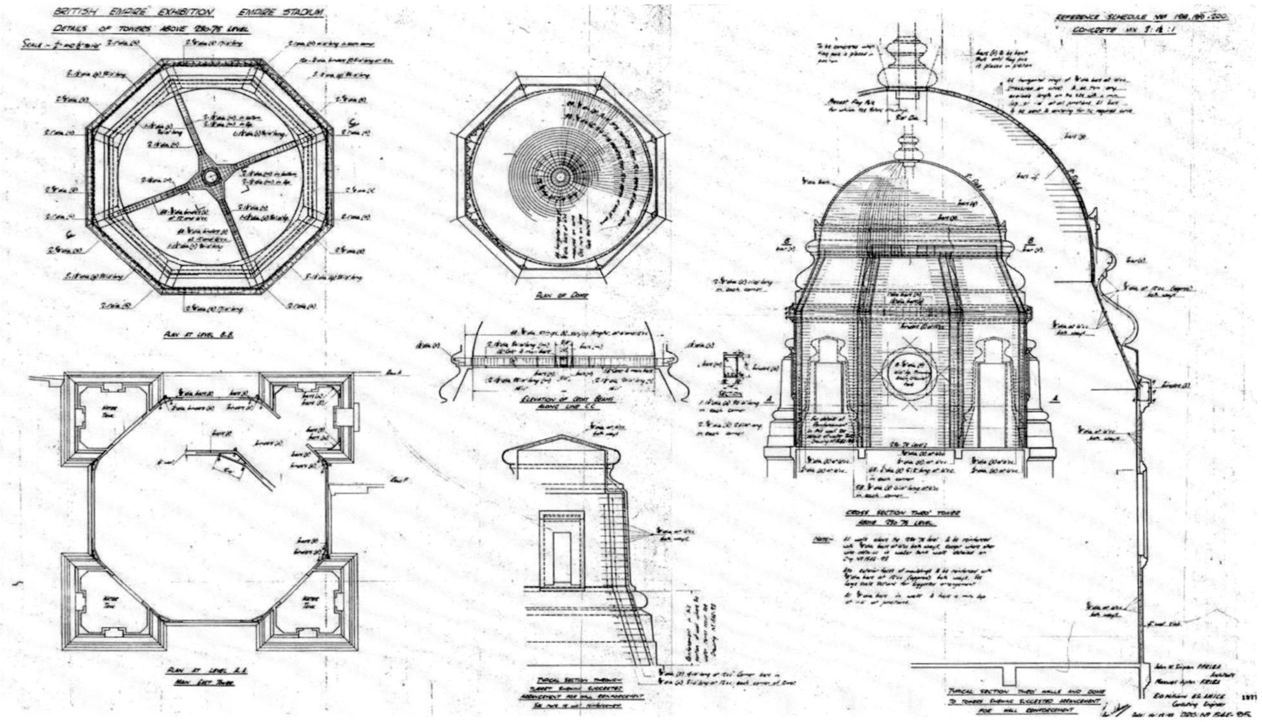

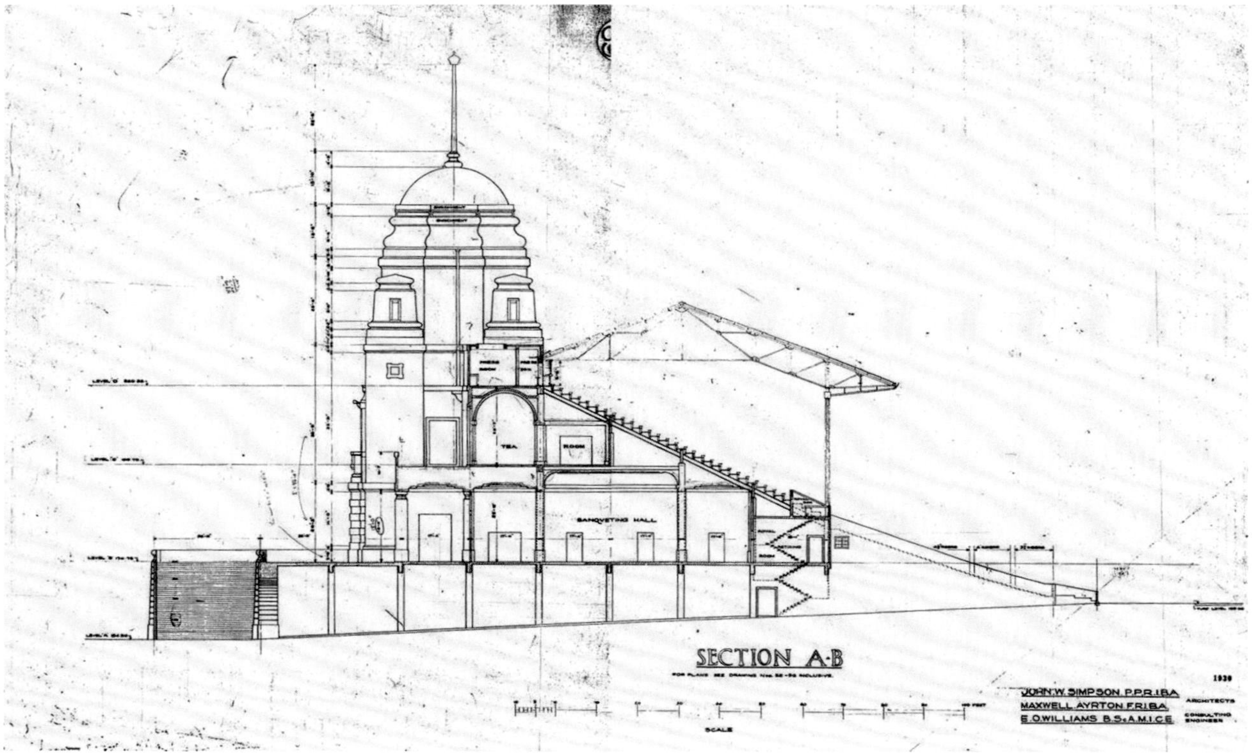

Above — Original construction drawings for the old Wembley Stadium's twin towers, whose design was influenced by Sir Edwin Lutyens' Viceroy's House in New Delhi. In common with all the buildings designed for the British Empire Exhibition, the towers were constructed entirely from reinforced concrete. The stadium itself required some 25,000 tonnes of concrete, but took just 300 days to complete.

Opposite — Wembley's towers under construction in 1922. The towers' domes were engineered to very fine tolerances – their ferro-concrete shells being just 75 millimetres deep.

The exhibition finally closed for good on 31 October 1925. There was no strategy in place for the future use of the site and most of the buildings had not been designed for long-term use. Eventually the land was sold privately to a speculator for £300,000 and most of the structures – which had cost over £2 million to build – were quickly dismantled. The massive Palaces of Industry, Engineering and Arts were retained and converted for industrial use. Of these, only a small part of the Palace of Industry survives today, along with the Wembley Arena, built to Owen Williams' designs in 1933-1934 as the Empire Pool.

Wembley Stadium, as completed in 1924, was a building of limited architectural interest. Set on the highest part of the site, it was aligned east-west to make optimum use of the available land, with a principal frontage – featuring the 38-metre-high 'twin towers' that were subsequently to become the symbol of Wembley – addressing Kingsway to the north. The design of the towers was clearly influenced by the dome of Lutyens' Viceroy's House in New Delhi, but the facade was executed entirely in concrete, jointed to resemble traditional masonry – a classic sham. The most remarkable aspect of the towers was the economy of their construction, their concrete shells measuring just 75 millimetres deep. During the First World War, their designer Owen Williams had worked on the design of concrete-hulled ships and this doubtless informed his work at Wembley.

The remainder of the stadium was essentially utilitarian, with concrete terraces supported on a steel frame and enclosed by an external wall of concrete, relieved by arches and punctuated by stair towers. Behind the main frontage was a series of refreshment rooms, including the Long Bar (originally the Tea Room) and a banqueting hall with seating for up to 1,000 people. Williams defended the mix of materials used in the stadium: 'It has been my guiding principle to use no material where another material would better serve', he told a gathering of engineers. 'To have used concrete where concrete should not be used would, apart from bad engineering, be of no service to the material itself.'

Not all critics were convinced. The engineer Oscar Faber wrote that the stadium 'looks well from the outside at a little distance. The inside was the roughest-looking concrete job I had seen for some time'. Faber concluded: 'the result does not represent what can be done, and while it is a milestone on the road towards the proper use of concrete, it is by no means the last milestone'. Faber was doubtless comparing Williams' work at Wembley with the far more innovative work in concrete of Eugène Freyssinet, Auguste Perret, Robert Maillart and others in Europe; and within a few years, Williams' almost exact contemporary, Pier Luigi Nervi, demonstrated the real potential of concrete for stadium design in his first great work, the Stadio Giovanni Berta in Florence.

However, it must be understood that Williams' achievement was not about refined design but about getting the exhibition buildings completed on time. The stadium itself was constructed in just 300 working days and was ready for use by spring 1923, a year ahead of the scheduled opening of the Empire Exhibition.

On 28 April 1923 the new stadium hosted its first FA Cup Final between Bolton Wanderers and West Ham United. The Football Association (founded in 1863) had identified the new stadium from the start as a venue for the grand finale of the English football season. With the tradition that the Cup Final should be held on neutral ground long established, and with Cup Finals attracting attendances of up to 100,000, the attractions of Wembley were obvious.

The earliest Finals – the first was in 1872, with a crowd of only 2,000 – had been held at Kennington Oval. Later, when the Surrey County Cricket Club decided that the event had outgrown their ground, numerous venues in London and the provinces were used. In 1895 the FA settled on Crystal Palace. However, facilities there were far from ideal and during the First World War, when no FA Cup Finals took place, the site was requisitioned as a munitions depot (Crystal Palace athletics stadium now stands on the site.)

In 1921 the FA signed a contract stating that Cup Finals would be held at Wembley initially for the next 21 years. As completed in 1923, the stadium accommodated 126,500 spectators, the great majority of them standing. Covered stands on the north and south sides of the stadium contained seats for 25,000. The 1923 Final – the famous 'White Horse' Final – was a potential disaster, with up to 200,000 people somehow squeezing into the stadium and eventually overflowing on to the pitch. (Nearly 150,000 came via Wembley Park station, substantially rebuilt for the Empire Exhibition.) Fortunately nobody was hurt but every subsequent FA Cup Final became an all-ticket event.

The 1923 Final revealed some deficiencies in the stadium: four extra stair towers were quickly added to ease the flow of spectators. The second Wembley Final took place three days after the opening of the exhibition, when nearly 92,000 people watched Aston Villa play Newcastle. During the summer months of 1924, the stadium hosted choral festivals, boy scout gatherings, firework displays, a Pageant of Empire, with 12,000 performers, and the highly popular Great International Rodeo, with 'cowboys from all over the world' and displays of steer roping, which attracted the wrath of the RSPCA.

Opposite — The legendary 'White Horse' FA Cup Final of 1923 – the first to be held at Wembley. Some 200,000 fans crowded into a stadium designed to accommodate 126,500. When His Majesty King George V took his place in Wembley's royal box, three-quarters of the field was covered with fans. Incredibly, mounted police were eventually able to clear the pitch and the game commenced.

After the closure of the exhibition, the stadium's commercial future appeared as uncertain as that of the other retained structures on the site, with which it formed a job lot. Ironically, it was the demolition contractor Arthur Elvin (1899-1957) who was responsible for securing the future of the stadium, which he bought for £122,500 in 1926 following the suicide of 'Jimmy' White, the speculator who had acquired the site but subsequently gone bankrupt. Elvin (a veteran of the First World War and aged just 27) formed a syndicate of investors, Wembley Stadium Ltd, to run the stadium, well aware that year-round events were crucial to its financial viability.

A vital element in the new management regime was the launch of the stadium as a venue for greyhound racing, which became a mass spectator sport during the inter-war period. From 1929 the Rugby League Cup Final was staged at Wembley and for some years speedway racing attracted large crowds. In total, a package of events was assembled that made the stadium pay its way. The nearby Empire Pool was commissioned by Elvin as an additional attraction – Edward Watkin's idea of Wembley as a centre of entertainment and recreation for the whole of London was re-emerging.

The decision that London should host the 1948 Olympic Games, the first to be staged after the Second World War, gave the stadium yet another role. London, which had been the venue for the 1908 Olympics, was scheduled to host the Games in 1944, but the war intervened. The late 1940s in Britain was a period of austerity; food was rationed and building work strictly controlled. With new construction ruled out, existing venues – including the Wembley Empire Pool (the last time it was used as a competition pool) and the Palace of Engineering (used for fencing) – were pressed into use. There was no Olympic Village: competitors were housed in private homes or a former military barracks and were even asked to bring their own supplies. Over 4,000 athletes from 59 countries participated, although Germany and Japan were not invited.

Wembley Stadium Ltd did its bit by providing free use of the stadium. Restrictions on building work were relaxed to allow modest improvements to the stadium, including new dressing rooms, bench seats in the former standing areas and an improved link to Wembley Park station. The running track, which had been submerged under the greyhound racing circuit, had to be excavated and relaid with 800 tonnes of cinders. At the eastern end of the stadium a platform was constructed to hold the Olympic Flame. The Games, the first ever Olympics to be televised, albeit for a tiny audience, were reckoned a considerable success and a major boost to London's morale in the drab years after the war. They are best remembered in sporting history, perhaps, for the extraordinary achievement of a 30-year-old Dutch athlete and new mother Fanny Blankers-Koen, who took four gold medals and won the hearts of spectators, earning the affectionate nickname 'the Flying Housewife'.

In the following decade, the viability of the stadium as a purely commercial operation was again an issue. Dog racing and speedway both declined in popularity in the post-war years; and although Wembley remained significant in the world of football, as post-war austerity receded it increasingly looked a somewhat lacklustre venue. A change of control in 1960 at Wembley Stadium Ltd, with BET, the parent company of Associated Rediffusion Television, becoming the principal shareholder, opened the way for increased investment. In 1963 the north and south stands were reroofed and the seating at the east and west ends covered for the first time. A new press box was also provided – the importance of television as a source of income was increasingly recognised. Floodlighting (first introduced in 1955) allowed games to be played after dark and in poor light. The result of this investment was a change in Wembley's fortunes. The AC Milan vs Benfica European Cup Final was held there in 1963 and other European Cup matches followed; and, of course, the World Cup Final was famously staged there in 1966.

The history of football in the last quarter century has been one of radical change. Twenty-five years ago, it was a game of limited appeal to the affluent and socially aspiring. Football grounds then were uncomfortable places, where a large proportion of spectators, then almost exclusively male, stood throughout the match, often in the open air. Toilet and refreshment facilities were primitive. Ticket prices, on the other hand, were comparatively low. The potential of television to provide a source of new income for the football industry and creating, potentially, a global audience was of huge significance. The establishment of the English Premier League in 1992 was a milestone – by the 2004-2005 season, the 20 clubs in the League were generating an income of £1.3 billion annually. Fans attending matches were prepared to pay higher prices for their tickets and demanded better facilities in return.

There were other, more tragic, facts behind the transformation of Britain's football grounds that began in the early 1990s. First, the Bradford disaster of 1985, in which a fire in a timber stand claimed the lives of 56 spectators, then the Hillsborough disaster of 1989, which left 96 Liverpool fans dead, led to far more stringent safety standards and all-seater stadiums became mandatory. The Heysel Stadium riot in Brussels in 1985 also had a huge impact. Major clubs invested heavily in new grounds, their comfortable seats, bars and restaurants a world away from the rain-soaked terraces of the 1970s.

Opposite — The British Empire Exhibition of 1924 was intended to showcase the best of industry, engineering and the arts from Britain and its 'Dominions and Colonies'. Featured here in a special section of *The Times* for Saturday 21 May 1924 is one of the fifteen avenues in the Palace of Engineering, a building constructed on a massive scale. The neighbouring Wembley amusement park was described as 'the last word in sensations'.

British Empire Section.] THE TIMES, SATURDAY, MAY 24, 1924. ix.

The Times.

BRITISH EMPIRE EXHIBITION

Special Section No. 2.

FROM THE EMPIRE'S WORKSHOPS—A VIEW IN ONE OF THE FIFTEEN AVENUES IN THE PALACE OF ENGINEERING.

01

02

03

04

05

01 On 1 August 1924, 12,253 boy scouts descended on the Empire Stadium for their Imperial Jamboree. Here, dressed in the warrior costume of Native American Indians, scouts file out of the arena.

02 From 14 June to 5 July 1924 the Empire Stadium became a Wild West Ranch with daily performances including bronco and bareback riding, steer wrestling and fancy roping.

03 HRH The Prince of Wales, left, accompanied by Lord Baden-Powell, inspects a boy scout troop at the Imperial Jamboree.

04 A contingent from the British Amateur Weight Lifters Association at Wembley for the National Festival of Youth, July 1937.

05 WL Tibberts wins the two mile race at the Oxford and Cambridge versus Yale and Harvard University Athletics meet at Wembley Stadium, July 1923.

From 1960 onwards, Wembley Stadium generated developments in the surrounding area that were not directly linked to football. The Esso Motor Hotel (later the Hilton) opened in 1971, followed, six years later, by the Wembley Conference Centre. Neither was architecturally significant, but they were seen as reinforcing Wembley's position as a focus for economic growth. The stadium itself, though, remained a period piece in a changing world, much loved but patently failing to match the standard set by other international venues. At one point, its deficiencies made the FA seriously consider the possibility of developing a new stadium on a site near Watford, where there was also space for a football training school and offices. However, the option was rejected, perhaps on sentimental as much as rational grounds – leaving Wembley was unthinkable.

By 1990, the year that Nelson Mandela was rapturously welcomed to Wembley, shortly after his historic release from political confinement, the stadium had become an all-seat venue, with a maximum capacity of 78,000. Wembley plc, as the owners were then known, had invested substantially in improvements to the stadium during the late 1980s and early 1990s. Changes to the stadium included: seating for an additional 4,000 people in a new 'Olympic Gallery' cleverly inserted below the roof of the existing seating bowl, together with a series of 12-seat private boxes; new medical facilities; refurbished public areas and additional toilets. However, it was still not enough; and it was not clear where the impetus, and funding, needed to transform Wembley could be found. Wembley plc was not prepared, or able, to invest more in the stadium, and the FA was merely an occasional tenant.

The catalyst that generated the new stadium was found in the National Lottery, established in 1993 with a commitment to fund 'good causes' – charities, the arts, the heritage, and sport. The principle of the Lottery was to provide money for those things that enriched the nation's life but could never be adequately provided for through taxation. The need for a modern 'national stadium' was self-evident and it was an obvious candidate for funding. The decision about its location, though, was less clear cut. Although London seemed to be the natural choice – Twickenham, for example, had been expensively reconstructed as the national venue for rugby union – provincial cities could not be discounted and the prospect of Lottery funding generated interest from a number of them.

A steering group set up by the then Sports Council included representatives from football, rugby league and athletics bodies. The new stadium would have to cater for both field and track events. During 1995 Birmingham, Bradford and Sheffield joined Manchester and London (in the form of Wembley) as contenders for the development, which was estimated to cost between £100 and £200 million and would accommodate 80,000 people, the cost to be partly provided by the Lottery. Wembley, in fact, was only added to the list after Wembley plc undertook to surrender the freehold of the stadium to a charitable trust – English National Stadium Trust – should the bid succeed. In return they secured a contractual agreement guaranteeing that the FA Cup Final and other major sporting events would be held there. By the autumn of that year, Birmingham, Bradford and Sheffield had all been ruled out and the choice lay between Manchester and Wembley. Manchester already had plans by Norman Foster for a proposed Olympic stadium, which it was felt could be revised and updated.

The idea of a national stadium was attractive, but it raised a critical issue – how do you create a stadium that is ideally suited for both football and athletics? A permanent running track would provide an unacceptable gulf between the pitch and spectators at a football match, it was argued; and, in any case, major athletics events were infrequent and attracted relatively small crowds. Although there were ways in which the problem could be addressed – a track concealed by retractable seating, for example, was being installed, at considerable cost, at Paris's new Stade de France – the football lobby felt unhappy about the provision for athletics.

In December 1996, when Wembley was named as the location for the new National Stadium, this and many other issues remained to be resolved. Would the new stadium cater equally for athletics and other sports, in line with the Sports Council's recommendations? How could the old stadium, a listed building, be wholly or partly demolished? Who would own and run the new stadium? How would funding in addition to the Lottery grant be raised? Finally, could the mystique of 'Wonderful Wembley' survive the process of rebuilding? Everything was still in play.

The British Empire Exhibition … has an opportune significance. It is a striking demonstration of the remarkable variety of people and resources which are found in that great Commonwealth of Nations known as the British Empire.

Prime Minister Ramsay MacDonald — *The Times*, 23 April 1924

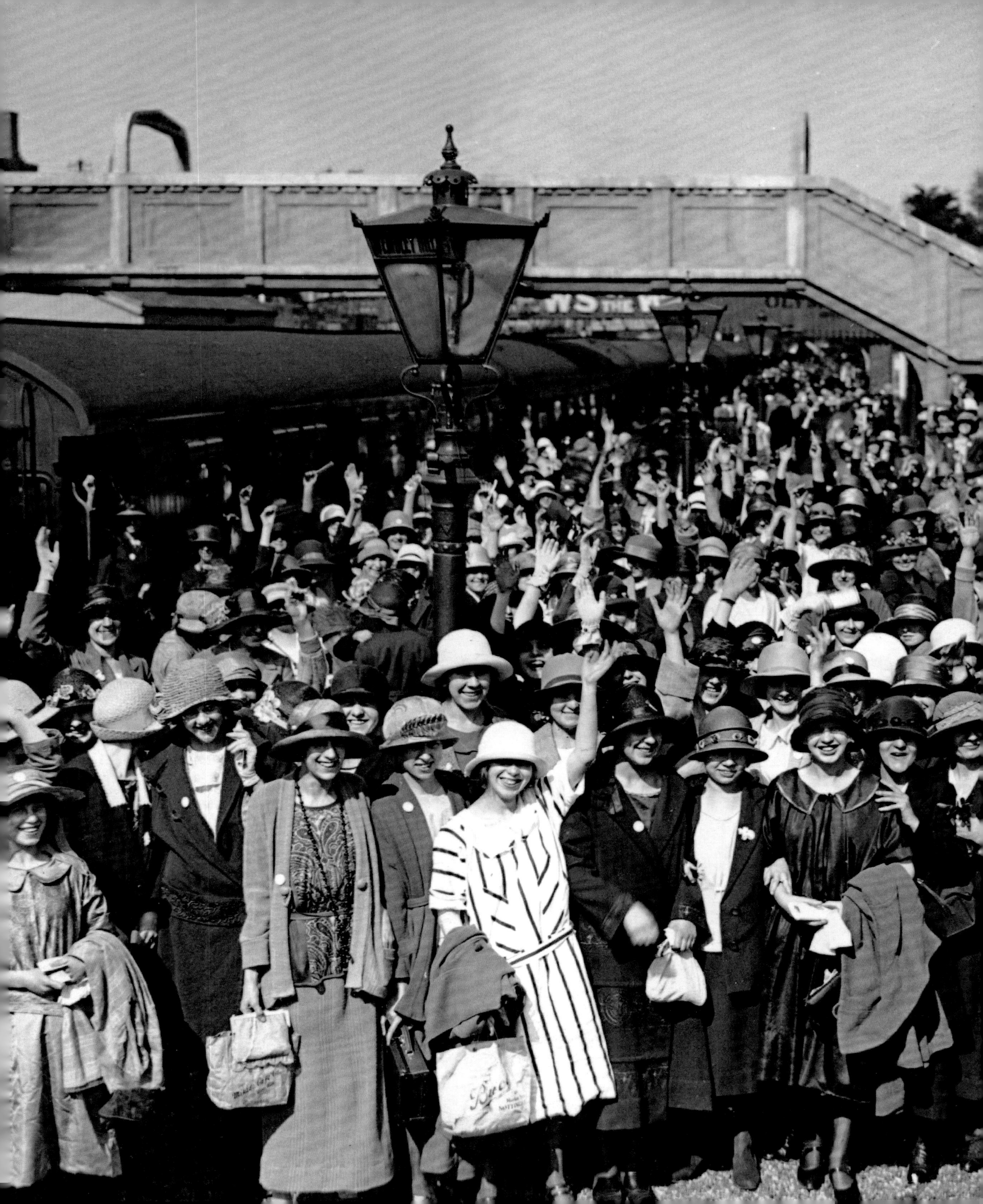

01

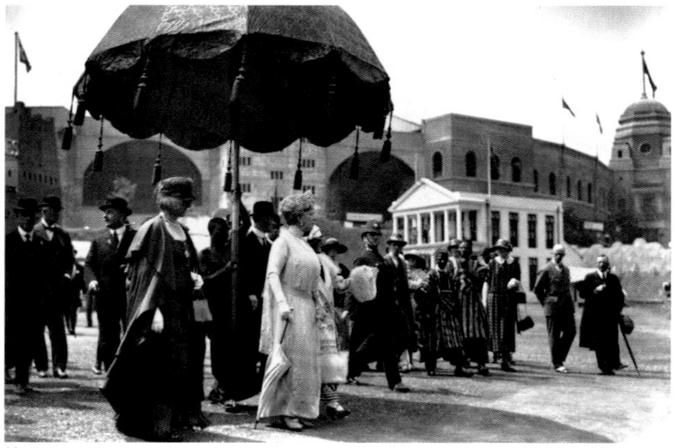

02

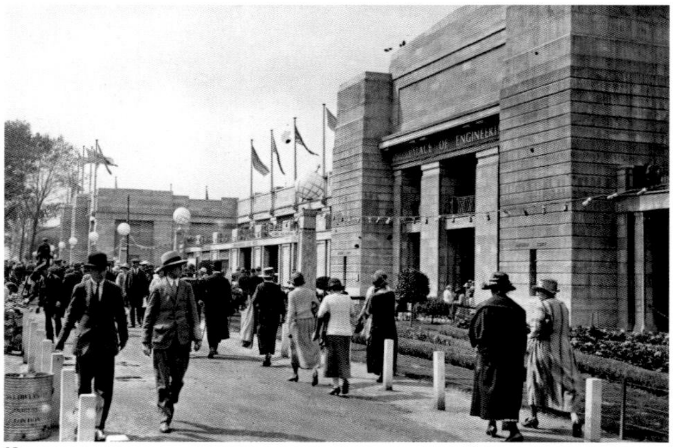

03

Wembley has arisen with its great pavilions as a shrine of Empire: it has become the natural meeting-place for the peoples of the British nations in every corner of the globe. Every day sees an increase in the crowds of people from London, from all over these islands, from the Dominions and Colonies, and from foreign parts who flock through the gates, and for each section of visitors the Exhibition has its special lesson.

THE TIMES, 24 MAY 1924

Previous page — Some of Boots the Chemist's 5,000 employees enjoying a day out at 'Wonderful Wembley', June 1924.

01 The pavilions for the British Empire Exhibition, nearing completion. The Indian pavilion is in the foreground and behind, from left to right, are those of Canadian Pacific, Canada and Australia. The Empire Stadium, as it was known then, occupied the highest part of the site.

02 Her Majesty Queen Mary is shown around the British Empire Exhibition on the opening day, 23 April 1924. The exhibition attracted some 17 million visitors in its first summer, proving so popular that it reopened the following year, finally closing on 31 October 1925.

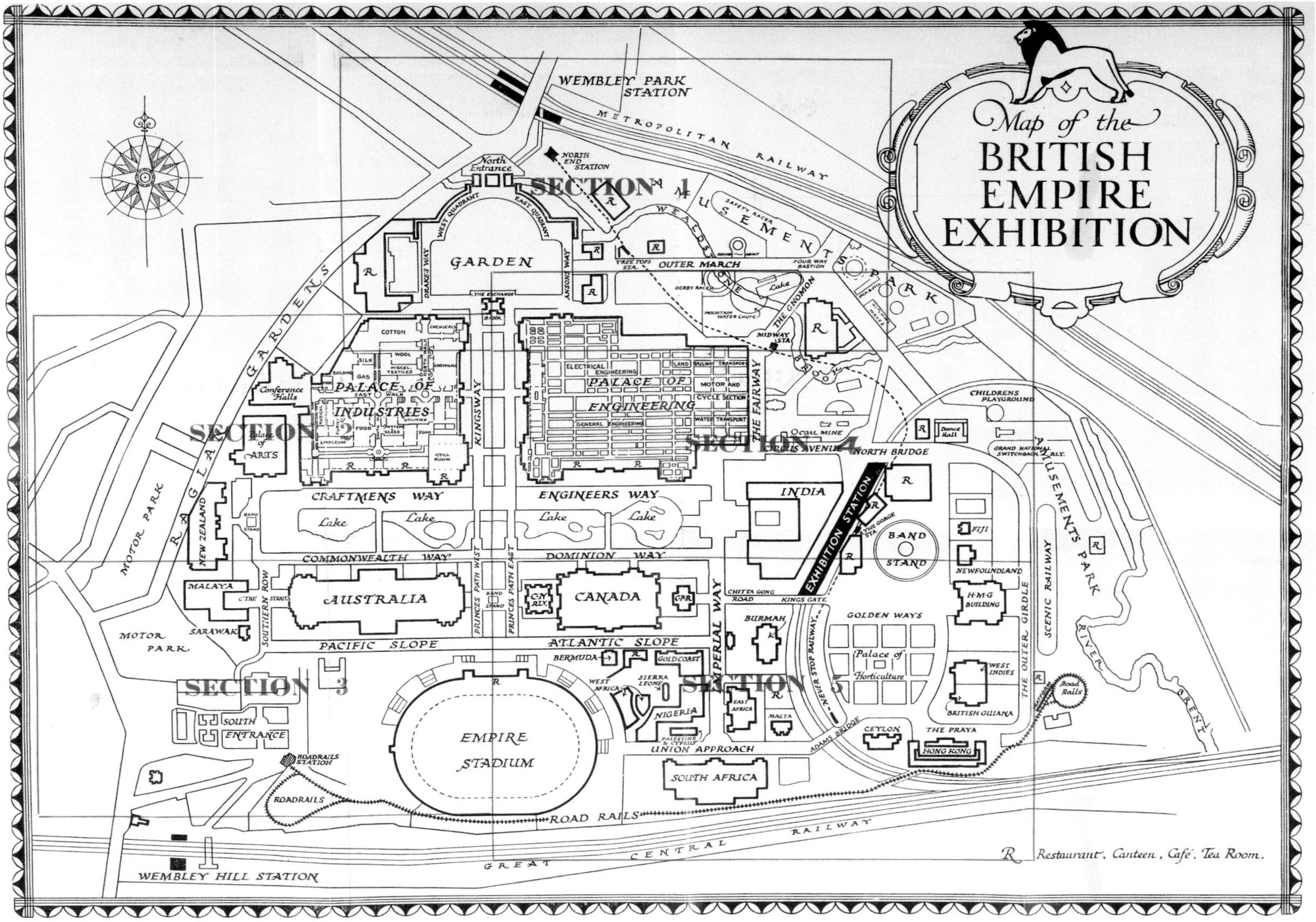

04

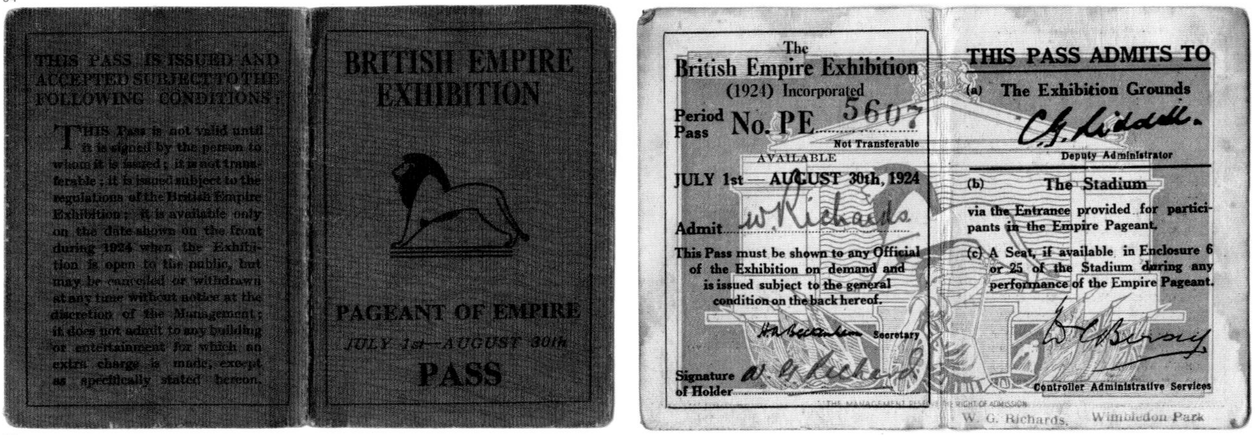

05

03 Looking towards the Palace of Engineering at the British Empire Exhibition. The building covered 5 hectares and was paired with the Palace of Industry, built on a similar scale. Together they showcased almost every aspect of British manufacturing and commerce.

04 A map of the British Empire Exhibition, taken from the official guidebook. The grounds covered 87 hectares and contained 'a hundred gates to the Empire'. Among thousands of exhibits were tropical gardens, palm groves, ostrich farms, goldfields, plantations of rubber, cotton, tea and coffee, flanked by vast palaces showcasing the Empire's industrial might.

05 An original pass to the British Empire Exhibition. The admission fee to the grounds was just one shilling and sixpence.

01

02

03

04

It is a family party, to which every member of the Empire is invited, and at which every part of the Empire is represented. INTRODUCTION TO THE OFFICIAL GUIDE TO THE BRITISH EMPIRE EXHIBITION, 1924

01 An aerial view of the Empire Stadium and the Australian pavilion, which was noted for eccentricities such as its display of scoured wool – a 16-foot ball sourced from every State and district in Australia – and its giant 1.5 tonne wheel of cheese.

02 Said to be the largest concrete building in the world at the time, covering six and a half times the size of Trafalgar Square, the Palace of Engineering displayed the wares and inventions of Britain's leading firms.

03 Visitors to the British Empire Exhibition crossed a recreation of Old London Bridge. Exotic delights such as the Burmese pavilion, seen to the right, with its gilded bells and lacquered interiors proved irresistible.

04 The Palace of Arts was visited by over two million people, each of whom paid sixpence to see various artistic and design endeavours, including works by Hogarth, Reynolds, and Gainsborough and bookbinding and printing developments since William Morris' Kelmscott Press.

05

06

07

08

09

05 Crowds greet the arrival of King George V and Queen Mary at the inauguration of the British Empire Exhibition, 23 April 1924. King George's opening dedication for 'the unity and prosperity of all my peoples and the peace and well-being of the world' was telegrammed 80 kilometres in eighty seconds, and the ensuing recording would be heard in many countries never reached before.

06 The Palace of Beauty, sponsored by soap manufacturer Pears, housed models who posed as famous beautiful women in history, among them Helen of Troy and Mary Queen of Scots, with costumes and backgrounds to match.

07 With delicacies such as birds' nests, shark's fin and mushrooms on the menu, the 150-seat restaurant in the Hong Kong pavilion provided a new culinary sensation to the British audience.

08 The Duke and Duchess of York, later King George VI and Queen Elizabeth, in a cable car at the Wembley Exhibition, 1925.

09 Onlookers line the bridge over one of the ornamental lakes between the Stadium and main Exhibition buildings. For the sum of one shilling visitors could take a tour of the lakes or 'travel from India to New Zealand on a summer afternoon'.

Overleaf — An aerial view of Wembley in the 1920s.

Oh bygone Wembley, where's the pleasure now?
The temples stare, the empire passes by.

JOHN BETJEMAN ON WEMBLEY, METRO-LAND, BBC TV, 1973

PIANOS
REFRIGERATING MACHINES

When the Briton thinks of the Olympic Games he thinks of the running ... and Mrs. Blankers-Koen from Holland, with her orange shorts and her fair floating hair, striding home time and again to victory, with all the irresistible surge of the great men sprinters, and stealing half their thunder.

The Times, 18 August 1948

USA
1
3

01

02

03

Previous page — Fanny Blankers-Koen of the Netherlands stands on the podium after winning gold in the women's 200-metre final of the 1948 Olympic Games. Great Britain's Audrey Williamson took silver and USA's Audrey Patterson took bronze.

01 A poster for the 1948 Olympic Games, depicting the arrival of the Olympic torch at Wembley. Despite the fear of Britain's rationed athletes appearing as 'scarecrows in running shoes', the 1948 Olympic Games proved a welcome distraction from post-war austerity.

02 The torch-bearer arrives at Wembley for the opening ceremony, bearing the flame carried from Olympia.

03 A poster for the 1948 Olympic Games. The hands of the Big Ben point to 4 o'clock, the time at which the opening of the Games was planned. The statue in the foreground is Discobolus, the discus thrower from Ancient Greece.

04

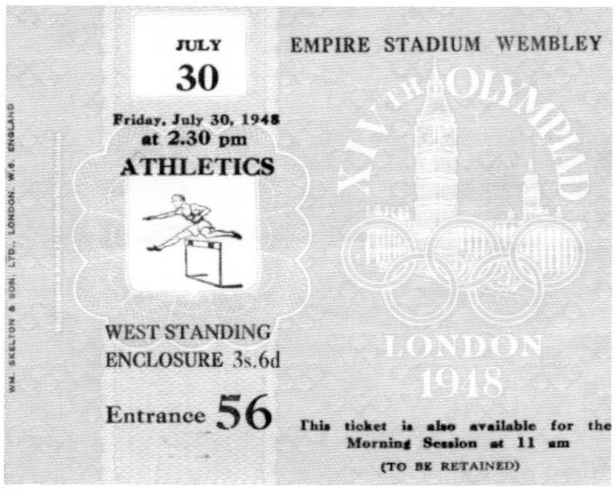

05

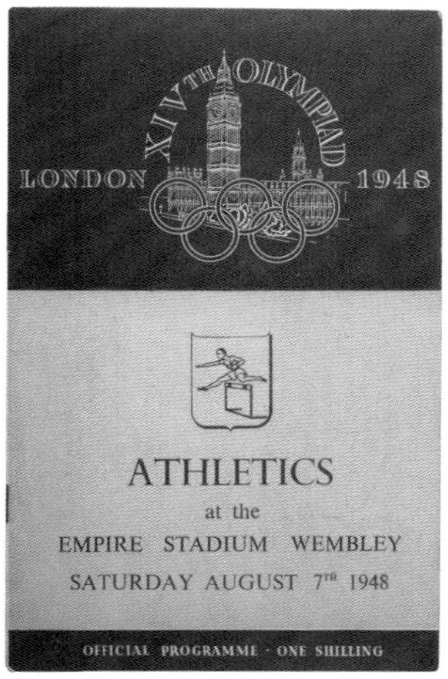

06

07

04 Athletes parade around the Empire Stadium during the opening ceremony of the Olympic Games, 28 July 1948. No new facilities were available for athletes; the men were housed in army barracks and the women in dormitories close to Wembley.

05 An admission ticket for the Olympic athletics events, dated 30 July 1948.

06 The cover of the official programme for the Olympic athletics events, 7 August 1948.

07 The opening day of the XIV Olympiad at Wembley Stadium, 29 July 1948. The Games hosted a record-breaking 5,980 athletes and officials from sixty nations.

01

02

03

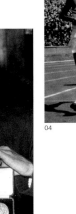

04

05

I was lucky enough to have been taken to see the 1948 Olympic games by my father, They were drab days, of course, in 1948, after the war, and the Olympics made a big difference to everyone. I can clearly remember the atmosphere inside Wembley, it inspired me to pursue a lifetime of active sport. ALAN KEEN, MP

01 An aerial view of the men's 100-metre final won by Harrison Dillard from the USA. Inspired by Jesse Owens, Dillard is the only American male to have won Olympic titles in both sprinting and hurdling to date.

02 The 10,000-metre final, won by Emil Zátopek of Czechoslovakia. The 'Locomotive', as he came to be known, dominated long distance running for six years from1948, winning thirty-eight consecutive 10,000-metre races and setting eighteen world records.

03 Fanny Blankers-Koen of the Netherlands – nicknamed the 'Flying Housewife' – takes the last flight of hurdles to win the 80-metre race in a world record time of 11.2 seconds. The mother of two, who listed 'housework' among her hobbies, became a favourite figure of the 1948 Olympics.

06

07

08

09

04 Runners leave Wembley Stadium at the start of the 1948 Olympic marathon led by Argentina's Guinez.

05 The thirty-year-old Blankers-Koen with three of her four gold medals for the 100- and 200-metre running finals and the 80-metre hurdles. Her training success was put down to a healthy diet, two hours training and three pints of milk daily.

06 The marathon, which was described as one of the most punishing courses ever selected for the Olympic Games, concluded in a heart-breaking finish for the leader, Etienne Gailly of Belgium, who failed in spectacular fashion half a lap short of gold.

07 American decathlete, Robert Mathias, throwing the discus at Wembley during the 1948 Olympics. The seventeen-year-old became the youngest winner in men's athletic history, despite misunderstanding several key decathlon rules.

08 Alberto Vallés was one of the three-man Mexican team which won the Olympic Prix De Nations competition at Wembley, August 1948.

09 After a tough race on a wet and heavy track, 1500-metre winner Henry Eriksson of Sweden is congratulated by the Wembley crowd. Eriksson contributed to Sweden's impressive forty-five medal tally, sixteen of which were gold.

01

02

03

04

05

06

'Heavens the noise! It is like ten million mechanical drills performing in unison. It swells and falls as the riders take the corners; it echoes about the cavernous concrete halls, drowning the feeble acclamations of the crowd; it dies slowly as the riders stop, and the end of a race seems like the end of a battle. It is titanic and terrible and monstrous; and yet in that enormous place, made by those monsters, it seems appropriate and right. And I do believe I rather liked it.' AP HERBERT, 1928

01 Speedway at Wembley: Jack Parker (left), captain of the English speedway team, and Frank Arthur, captain of the Australian team, before a race at Wembley Stadium, 1932.

02 Eighteen-year-old speedway rider Buster Brown takes a corner at speed during a race track meeting at Wembley, 1949.

03 Buster Brown chats with Wembley trainer, Alec Jackson, before a speedway track event, 1949.

04–06 Souvenir programmes for the second Speedway Test Match, England v Australia at Wembley, 1952; the third Speedway Test Match, England v Australia, 1951; and the Speedway Championship of the World Final at Wembley, 1952.

Opposite — Making way for speedway. Turf is removed from the Wembley pitch in preparation for a National League Competition race between the Wembley and Crystal Palace speedway teams, 1933.

01

02

03

04

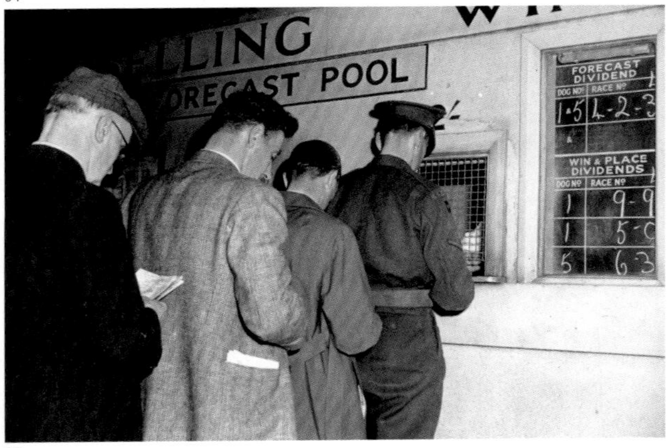

05

06

01 Racing greyhounds are exercised in the grounds of Wembley Stadium, shaded from the heat by a large umbrella, 1936.

02 In the late 1920s, in order to diversify Wembley's use and increase profits, entrepreneur Arthur Elvin introduced new sports including greyhound racing on a weekly basis. The first night of dog racing on 10 December 1927 attracted 50,000 people. In one memorable incident a dog caught and savaged the mechanical hare.

03 Greyhounds about to enter the traps, 1932. Wembley was the premier venue for the sport until the final race in 1998.

04, 05 Queues form at the betting window of the Tote, 1945. Football had made Wembley famous but from the late 1920s onwards the dogs paid the rent.

07

08

09

06 Greyhound champion,'Model Dasher', leads the other competitors in a parade for the crowd before the start of a race, 1930.

07 A packed crowd survey the greyhound track at Wembley in the 1940s.

08 Dogs are released from the trap at Wembley, 1945. Cup Final afternoons were a flurry of activity as 20,000 seats were removed in preparation for the racing night ahead. Arthur Elvin recalls that 'the goal-posts disappeared before the last football fan had left the ground!'

09 Greyhound racing at Wembley in the 1960s. A refusal to cancel the regular greyhound race by Wembley's owners meant that the 1966 World Cup match between Uruguay and France was played at White City.

HENRY COOPER v CASSIUS CLAY — 1963
World Heavyweight Non-Title Fight

Clay is down!
Cooper has downed him!
Oh! A beautiful punch there!
And as the bell goes Clay has just been dropped …
What a beautiful punch from Cooper!

Simon Smith, BBC Commentator — 18 June 1963

AMPRO

Previous page — 'Enry's 'ammer' floors Cassius Clay as the bell sounds for the end of the fourth round of the heavyweight non-title fight. A controversial extended break allowed Clay to recover and emerge victorious in the fifth as he had predicted, 18 June 1963.

Above — Billy Graham's evangelical zeal draws a record crowd of 120,000 in 1954, the first of several such visits to Wembley.

Opposite — Pope John Paul II celebrates mass at Wembley in 1982.

People are dying NOW!
Give us the money now,
Give ME the money NOW!
Fuck the address,
just give the phone,
here's the number …

Bob Geldof, Musician and Live Aid Organiser — 13 July 1985

01

02

03

04

05

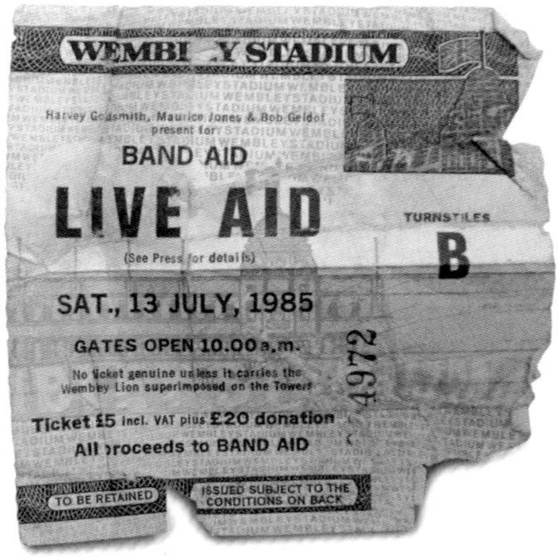

06

Previous page — The Live Aid concert crowd at Wembley Stadium on 13 July 1985. Live Aid was televised around the world and raised millions of pounds to help relieve severe famine in Ethiopia.

01 Rockin' all over the world: Status Quo kick off Live Aid – a 'global jukebox' of pop music that lasted sixteen hours.

02 The capacity Live Aid audience. The organiser's initial expectation to raise £1 million was dwarfed by the final figure of £150 million.

03 Bono woos the Live Aid crowd. U2's fledgling performance established them as a live act to contend with; as superstars they would fill Wembley Stadium many times over.

04 The Prince and Princess of Wales with Bob Geldof at the Live Aid concert. In recognition of his efforts, Geldof – an Irish citizen – received an honorary knighthood.

05 As temperatures soared into the thirties, security staff hosed down the sweltering Live Aid crowd.

06 A Live Aid ticket, Saturday 13 July 1985.

07

09

08

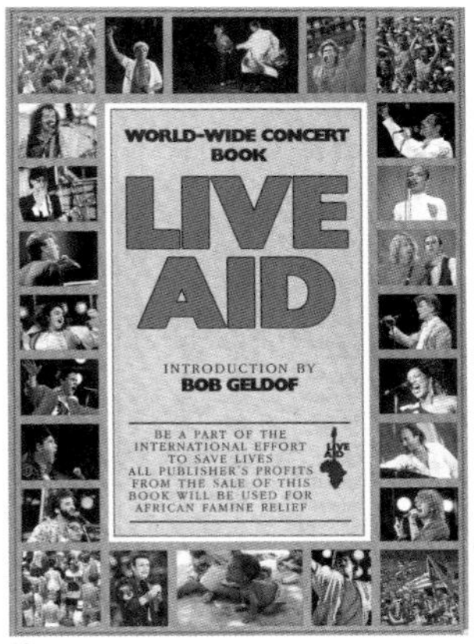

10

07 A sea of hands applauds the Live Aid show. One audience member recalls that 'it wasn't just about the show – there was a feeling that something significant was going happen'.

08 Bob Geldof unites Britain's biggest and best music stars for a Live Aid finale of 'Feed the World'.

09 Freddie Mercury, who stole the show at Live Aid.

10 The front cover of the Live Aid book, commemorating simultaneous concerts at JFK Stadium in Philadelphia, Pennsylvania, and Wembley Stadium in London.

Even through the thickness of the prison walls at Robben Island, Pollsmoor, Victor Verster, Pretoria, Kroonstad, Diepkloof and elsewhere, we heard your voices demanding our freedom.

Nelson Mandela — 16 April 1990

ANC

01

02

03

04

Previous page — Preceded by a six-minute-long ovation, Nelson Mandela addressed an ecstatic Wembley crowd, just a few weeks after his release from prison in Cape Town on 11 February 1990.

01 The Nelson Mandela concert at Wembley Stadium, 1990. Over a billion people across five continents watched on television as Mandela himself took the stage.

02 South African musicians perform to a receptive crowd at the Nelson Mandela concert.

03 African National Congress leader Nelson Mandela celebrates his freedom at Wembley. His then wife Winnie Mandela and ANC activist Adelaide Tambo look on.

04 The Wembley audience was stirred by Mandela's speech urging a continued and united offensive for the abolition of the apartheid system in South Africa.

05

06

07

08

09

10

11

Wembley has entertained audiences with a roll-call of who's who in music.

05–11 Mick Jagger performs for the Rolling Stones' Urban Jungle Tour at Wembley, 1990; David Bowie at the NetAid concert, 1999; the Rolling Stones in 1990; caricatures of U2's Bono and Adam Clayton at the Zooropa tour, 1993; Madonna's Girlie Show, 1993; Michael Jackson on the HIStory tour, 1997; The Three Tenors in Concert, 1996.

LEEDS v WIGAN — 1995
Rugby League Challenge Cup Final

The hooter goes and Wigan have won their eighth successive Challenge Cup Final!
Leeds haven't just been beaten today, they've been hammered into the ground at Wembley Stadium and the Leeds players know that.

Ray French, BBC Commentator — 29 April 1995

SPORT

01

02

03

Previous page — Martin 'Chariots' Offiah celebrates a try for Wigan against Leeds in the Challenge Cup Final at Wembley, 1995.

01 Rugby League at Wembley. From 1987 to 1995 the all-conquering Wigan were unbeaten in Wembley Rugby League Challenge Cup Finals. Here Wigan's Shaun Edwards is tackled by Hull's Peter Sterling in the Challenge Cup Final, 1985. Wigan beat Hull 28–24.

02 A triumphant Wigan team after their 32–12 Challenge Cup Final win against Halifax at Wembley, 1988.

03 Castleford versus Wigan on the field at the Challenge Cup Final, 1992.

04

06

07

05

08

04 Wigan captain, Dean Bell, holds the trophy aloft after the Challenge Cup Final against Widnes at Wembley, 1993.

05 Sam Panapa of Wigan celebrates victory in the Challenge Cup Final against Widnes at Wembley, 1993.

06 The last Rugby League Final at Wembley, 1999. The Leeds Rhinos faced the London Broncos and won the match 52–16.

07 Leeds Rhinos' four-try hero Leroy Rivett in action at the 1999 Challenge Cup Final. Rivett beats Broncos' Steele Retchless to score a corner try.

08 Leeds captain, Iestyn Harris, holds the trophy aloft with Rivett. As man-of-the-match, the winger's outstanding performance won him the Lance Todd Trophy.

VENUE OF LEGENDS

Patrick Barclay

The scene remains etched in many millions of minds. It was one of those for which time seems to stand still as much out of weariness as respect. Almost every participant in the World Cup Final was exhausted by a match that had gone into extra time and been all but settled by a goal whose legitimacy would be debated for ever.

The scorer of that goal was Geoff Hurst. Fate would give him the opportunity to make absolutely sure the English hosts in 1966 would triumph: to preclude any further twist such as that which Wolfgang Weber had given the plot by equalising for West Germany in the dying seconds of normal time. By completing a hat-trick, Hurst would make it 4–2.

Although World Cup Finals are notoriously tiring, especially for the side in arrears – four years later, the Italians were to be reduced to the role of panting observers as a peerless Brazil waltzed through them to score an unforgettably beautiful fourth goal – it cannot have been often that an attacker on such an important occasion has met such flimsy resistance as did Hurst; or, for that matter, been afforded such scanty support. While few Germans had the energy to try to stop him, there was hardly a fellow Englishman – with the notable exception of the 21-year-old Alan Ball, whose dogged and incisive running had been an influential factor in the drama's unfolding – with the legs to offer an option. Hurst went it alone. Somehow, for finding the strength to shoot, providence rewarded him with such sweet, clean contact that the ball flew in a blur past Hans Tilkowski, whose astonishment was understandable. As it happened, some of the 96,924 spectators had been on the pitch. We know because Kenneth Wolstenholme, commentating for BBC television, told us. 'They think it's all over,' he had continued, casually uttering one of the most memorable lines in the history of sports of commentary as Hurst drew back his foot. 'It is now!' What Wolstenholme said next – 'It's four!' – was lost in the commotion as football's birthplace prepared to celebrate its one and only moment of true, universal, supremacy in the game.

Was that Wembley's greatest moment? If you are English, you would probably think so. A German might not. A German might prefer to dwell on the year 2000 and the victory of his now-unified nation in the last match played at the stadium before it was rebuilt, when Didi Hamann put the only goal past David Seaman, and England's manager, Kevin Keegan, whose past associations with Germany had been so happy – twice, when at Hamburg in the late 1970s, he had been named as European Footballer of the Year – was so dismayed he resigned.

A Scot would recall 1967, when those world champions of Sir Alf Ramsey's were not only humbled under the twin towers but mercilessly taunted, Jim Baxter playing keepy-uppy as he teased Nobby Stiles. Or hark back to 1928, when the little 'Wembley Wizards' journeyed south to win 5–1. A Hungarian would think of 1953, when his countrymen came and conquered – it was the first time a team from outside Britain had done so – to the tune of 6–3, leaving the great English player Tom Finney to observe: 'They went into my personal memory file – and that of millions of other football-lovers – as the finest team ever to sort out the intricacies of this wonderful game'.

A Catalan would alight upon the evening in 1992 when Barcelona became club champions of Europe for the first time; they beat Sampdoria. A native of a less balmy coast would have just as little hesitation in plumping for 1973, when Sunderland of England's second division overcame the mighty Leeds United to win the FA Cup through a goal by Ian Porterfield and an astonishing save from Jimmy Montgomery. A neutral would pick from such upsets as that or Southampton's overcoming of Manchester United through a goal by Bobby Stokes in 1976 or the great Finals: 1948, when United overcame a Blackpool featuring Stanley Matthews (later to be knighted, like Finney, as a mark of the esteem in which the whole nation held him); or 1953, when Matthews returned with the seaside club and emerged victorious due to his setting up for Bill Perry of the afternoon's seventh goal; or 1987, when Coventry City beat Tottenham Hotspur 3–2 in a match remarkable for both the quality the teams displayed on the pitch and the friendliness with which their followers mingled off it (remember that the worst horrors of hooliganism remained all too fresh in the mind only two years after the carnage at the Heysel Stadium). Others might point to the unique drama of the play-offs and 1998, when Charlton scrambled into the Premiership on penalties after Clive Mendonca had contributed a hat-trick to a 4–4 draw.

But could any of these occasions surpass the night when Manchester United became the first English club to win the European Cup (as the forerunner to the Champions League was generally known)? It was in 1968, a decade after the air disaster that had claimed the lives of several members of a United first team regarded as potential European champions. The manager, Matt Busby, was seriously injured in the crash at Munich but had recovered and rebuilt the team. The whole nation knew how much it meant to him when United swept aside the challenge of Portugal's Benfica, the great Eusébio and all, under the twin towers. United had great players of their own and two of them scored in a 4–1 triumph after extra time, Bobby Charlton claiming two goals and George Best a typically audacious and elegant one. A photograph of Busby's post-match embrace with Best, whose off-the-field habits caused the pipe-smoking boss so much distraction – without diluting his affection for the young Northern Irishman – summarised the mixture of joy and relief released by the achievement, as did more tears from Charlton, who had cried on the same pitch as England had

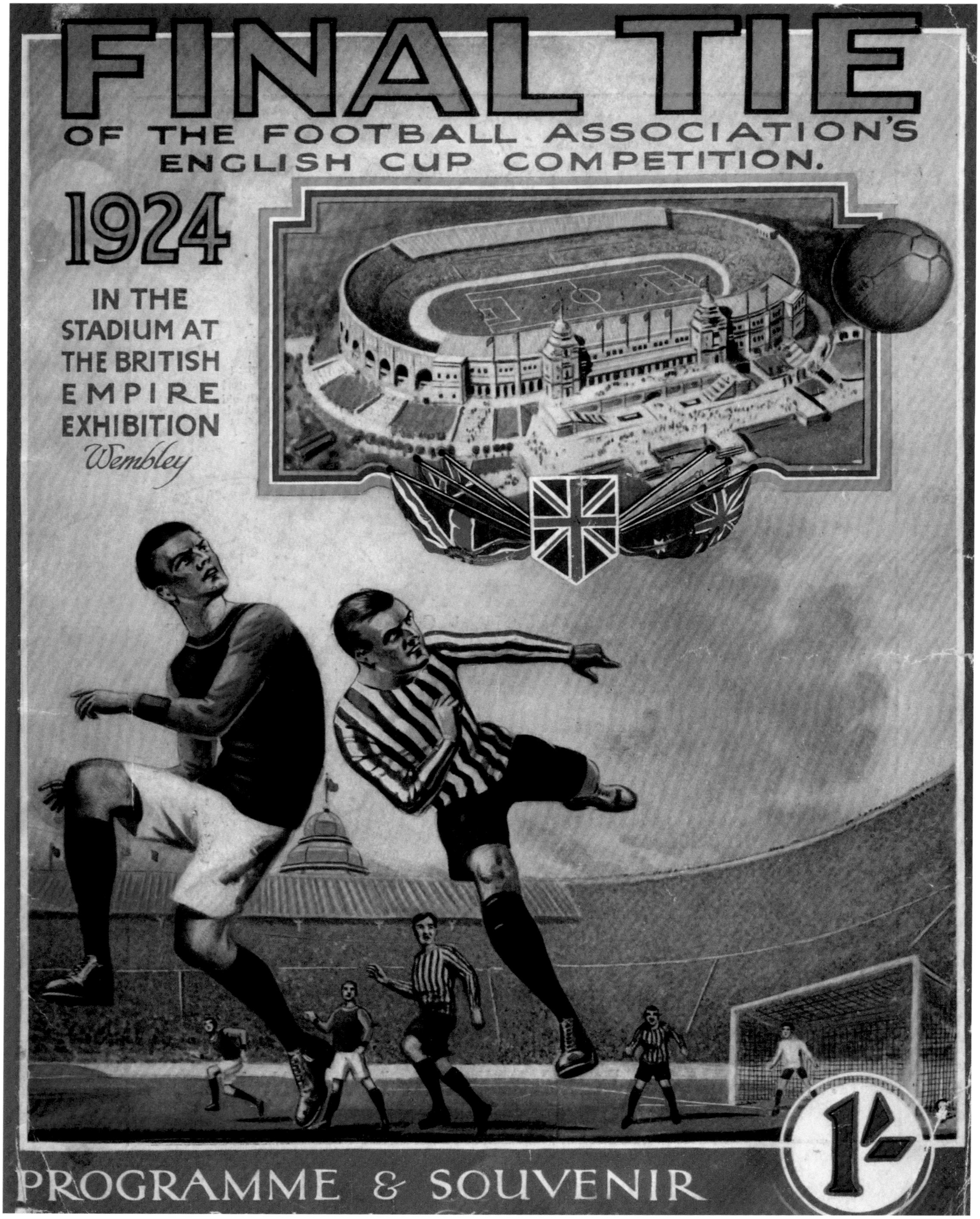
FINAL TIE
OF THE FOOTBALL ASSOCIATION'S
ENGLISH CUP COMPETITION.
1924
IN THE
STADIUM AT
THE BRITISH
EMPIRE
EXHIBITION
Wembley
1/-
PROGRAMME & SOUVENIR

taken the World Cup two years earlier. In 1978, Liverpool claimed their second consecutive European title with a more businesslike dispatching of Bruges, Graeme Souness making the only goal for Kenny Dalglish.

No reference to Wembley's hosting of European Finals could be complete without a salute to the achievement of West Ham in claiming the European Cup-Winners' Cup in 1965. A year after Bobby Moore had lifted the FA Cup, Preston North End having been beaten in the final, he returned to climb the 39 steps and receive the UEFA trophy. Two goals from the winger Alan Sealey had seen off Munich 1860 and once more 100,000 had been there to watch. There was, of course, to be a trio of West Ham players – not just Moore but Hurst and Martin Peters – in the stadium a year later as the captain clambered up to meet the Queen and, after a polite wipe of his shaking hand on his shorts, collect the ultimate trophy. Quite a hat-trick, rounded off in style.

The old stadium could not live on football alone and inhabitants of the Rugby League towns either side of the Pennines would have their fondest memories of that sport's annual day in the sun. A speedway fan might have other ideas and a greyhound punter might cherish the night he made a fortune. But overwhelmingly the Wembley story is of a wealth – an almost unfathomable wealth – of football.

From the morning the stadium opened, to be flooded by more than 200,000 demanding – and obtaining, quite roughly in many cases – admission to the inaugural FA Cup Final, to the dark evening some 77 years later when, England's vanquished footballers and the disconsolate Keegan having stolen out attracting as little attention as they could from stragglers taking a last look at the towers, its gates clanked shut, there has been such an unparalleled catalogue of drama as to make it difficult to know where to start. So let us try the beginning.

Cup Finals — from David Jack to David James

The official attendance at the 1923 Final was 126,047, but that number could have been accommodated on the slopes of the newly built arena, the biggest and most imposing in the world, without too much of a squeeze. The FA had seriously underestimated demand for the event and so many people had swept through the gates after the announcement that they had been closed at 1.45pm, an hour and a quarter before the scheduled kick-off. Then only the pitch was visible; even areas of that kept disappearing under the sea of heads that ebbed and flowed and would almost certainly have prevented play but for the skill of a police horse. Billy, ridden by Constable George Scorey, used his nose and famous white rump (actually grey, but it appeared white in newspaper photographs) to coax the hordes back to the touchlines.

It seems incredible that no one was killed and few injured in the crush – especially now, in the light of the terrible tragedy of 1989 at Hillsborough, where the 96 victims had gone in the hope of seeing Liverpool reach Wembley at Nottingham Forest's expense – but Scorey was modestly to ascribe this in part to the spectators' good humour. Witnesses told of being just carried around with their feet off the ground and, amusingly, of being able to hear but not see the band of the Irish and Grenadier Guards as they played on the pitch at 2.40. An hour later, Billy having done his work, the match between Bolton Wanderers and West Ham United began.

Bolton, a mid-table First Division side, was the favourite. West Ham had joined the League only four years earlier, on its resumption after the First World War, and remained in the Second Division, though they did secure promotion with a win at Sheffield Wednesday just two days after their defeat in the Final. Not surprisingly, they questioned the legitimacy of the Wembley outcome – in vain, while trailing in the second half, they had appealed to the referee for an abandonment – but Bolton reckoned they had won fair and square despite rumours that their winger Ted Vizard had received the benefit of a spectator's friendly foot in keeping the ball in play during the run down the left that preceded the second goal.

The first had been unusual in that West Ham's Jack Tresadern, after throwing in to Jack Young, became entangled with the crowd. Young's attempt at a clearance was intercepted by David Jack, whose fierce shot past Ted Hufton went down in history as the first Wembley goal. Hufton did not have to pick the ball from the net, which had been trampled underfoot; an unfortunate spectator had to absorb the impact of Jack's drive. Only as the Bolton players celebrated could Tresadern find his way back on to the pitch. Later Vizard's cross was volleyed by John Smith, the shot hitting the underside of the crossbar and bouncing down and, just as Geoff Hurst's was to do in 1966, getting the nod from the match officials. Bolton got their first major trophy. West Ham was to obtain the consolation of a step up the First Division. And the FA, while pocketing its share of world record receipts – £27,776 – for a sporting event, learned a lesson, announcing that the following season the FA Cup Final would be all-ticket and, of course, it has remained so.

Opposite — The cover of the1924 FA Cup Final programme and souvenir. It was the first all-ticket match FA Cup Final held at Wembley, lessons having been learned from the preceding year's mayhem.

While that first Final was remembered mainly for the extraordinary scenes that surrounded it, the occasion of 1948, in which Manchester United beat Blackpool 4–2, became one of the few cherished for the quality of its football. There had been a fine match in 1935, when Sheffield Wednesday beat West Bromwich Albion by the same score, but this had the critics purring with pleasure: even in advance, for both sides had reputations for playing handsome, enterprising football home and away.

At Old Trafford it had been Matt Busby's second season and his gift for building a team was already evident; United had finished second in the League. Blackpool ended ninth but featured the wing wizard Stanley Matthews, in his first season since coming from Stoke City, and another outstanding forward in Stan Mortensen. Before the match, tickets were changing hands at more than 100 times their face value. Nor were the public disappointed as, from the start, both teams attacked in turn. Blackpool led through Eddie Shimwell's disputed penalty; Jack Rowley equalised with a tap-in; Mortensen maintained his record of scoring in every round; Rowley did it again with a raging header amid further dispute (over the alacrity with which the preceding free-kick had been taken); and with 12 minutes left Stan Pearson cleverly set himself up for a shot that went in off a post, leaving John Anderson to make absolutely sure of United's first Wembley triumph for 39 years. The Busby era had begun in earnest. But the day's significance was as much its spirit; the Blackpool players generously applauded those who had denied them the trophy. Meanwhile it was frequently remarked that neither side deserved to lose. But the fact was that Matthews had five more years to wait for his winners' medal.

As in 1948, when he was rather outshone by Walter Rickett on the other wing, Matthews did not give one of his more dazzling displays and the true hero of the 1953 final, in many eyes, was the hat-trickster Mortensen. Yet the man for whom the people rooted was Matthews and, when his ball was put past the Bolton goalkeeper by Perry, it drew the country together in celebration of the veteran dribbler who, it turned out, was still to entertain audiences for many years.

What with Matthews and the transformation of Blackpool's fortunes – with three quarters of the match gone they had been 3–1 down – 1953 was a great Final. But often these supposed climaxes to the season were a disappointment, whether through the pressure on the players to perform, end-of-campaign tiredness or even (as was oddly ventured) the lushness of the Wembley pitch, which some thought exacerbated fatigue.

On several occasions injury cruelly depleted a side; a spate of these occurrences began with the Manchester City goalkeeper Bert Trautmann's broken neck in 1955. Another goalkeeper, Ray Wood of Manchester United, suffered a broken cheekbone in 1957. Then came the leg breaks sustained in successive years by Roy Dwight of Nottingham Forest in 1959 and Dave Whelan of Blackburn Rovers (later to become Wigan Athletic's chairman on their rise to the Premiership) in 1960, followed by the ankle damage that caused Len Chalmers of Leicester City to hobble almost throughout the 1961 match. Only Dwight was on the winning side. The argument for substitutes became deafening and in 1968 West Bromwich's Dennis Clarke became the first of those in an FA Cup Final, replacing John Kaye as the Albion beat Everton. A substitute's goal first won the Cup when Eddie Kelly helped Arsenal to the Double in 1971.

In the meantime there had been a classic Final in 1966, when Sheffield Wednesday performed brilliantly for an hour and led 2–0, only to tire and be overtaken by two goals from Everton's Mike Trebilcock – a rare footballer in that he was a Cornishman – and one, the winner, from Derek Temple. The trouble with that match was that it took place in the wrong year and the memory of it remains somewhat buried, except on Merseyside and in South Yorkshire.

A poorer match, but an even more thrilling culmination – among the most thrilling of any domestic Final – went the way of Arsenal in 1979, when a confrontation with Manchester United exploded into life and Liam Brady, with his socks rolled down, crossed for Alan Sunderland to settle matters at 3–2. It was the Highbury club's third Final of the decade and they were to return in a year to be shocked by a rare header from Trevor Brooking for West Ham of the Second Division which added the East London club's name to those of Sunderland and Southampton on the list of Wembley giant killers. In 1978, Arsenal had been wrong-footed by another unlikely winner, driven by Roger Osborne of Bobby Robson's Ipswich Town.

The centenary FA Cup Final in 1981 went to a replay in which the less celebrated of Tottenham Hotspur's Argentines, Ricky Villa, scored one of the most famous winners, weaving in from the left flank and bemusing several Manchester City defenders before squeezing the ball past Joe Corrigan. Steve MacKenzie suffered more than any other City player, for earlier in the match he had volleyed arguably an even better goal. That was the FA Cup Final's first Wembley replay and four years later more history was made when Kevin Moran became the first player to be sent off in the event,

01

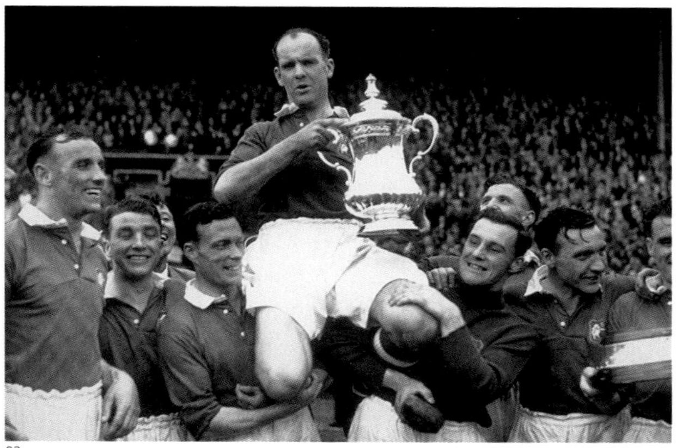

02

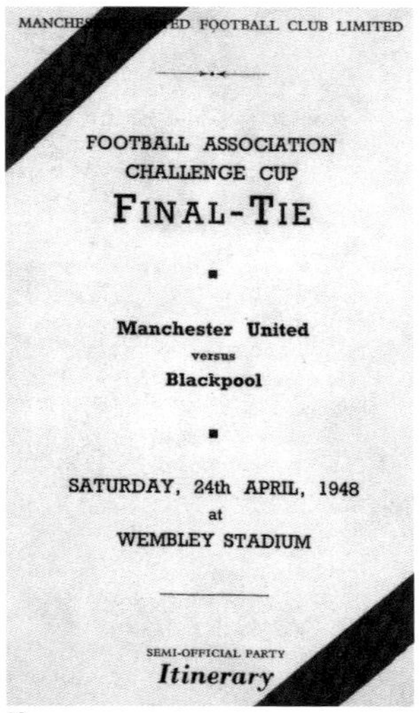

FOOTBALL CLUB LIMITED

FOOTBALL ASSOCIATION
CHALLENGE CUP
FINAL-TIE

Manchester United
versus
Blackpool

SATURDAY, 24th APRIL, 1948
at
WEMBLEY STADIUM

SEMI-OFFICIAL PARTY
Itinerary

03

04

01 The crowd in the Wembley stands watches the FA Cup Final between Manchester United and Blackpool, 1948.

02 Manchester United captain Johnny Carey is carried shoulder high after his team's 4–2 win against Blackpool in the FA Cup Final, 1948.

03 An itinerary issued to Manchester United giving the details of travel arrangements for the 'Semi-Official Party' of the FA Cup Final, 1948.

04 A 1948 FA Cup Final souvenir featuring the players and officials from both teams.

01

02

03

04

05

01 Scenes from the 1953 'Matthews' FA Cup Final – Blackpool versus Bolton Wanderers. Blackpool's Stan Mortensen falls to the ground as he scores his side's second goal on his way to completing a hat-trick. Blackpool beat Bolton Wanderers 4–3.

02 Blackpool's Stan Mortensen hammers in his first goal on his way to a hat-trick.

03 Bolton Wanderers' defenders look on in despair as Blackpool's outside-left Bill Perry (far right) scores the winning goal.

04 Blackpool's Stanley Matthews is chaired by team mates Jackie Mudie, left, and Stan Mortensen after collecting his winners' medal.

05 Stanley Matthews receives his FA Cup winners' medal from Her Majesty the Queen, the only major honour of his career.

the Manchester United defender having brought down Everton's Peter Reid; despite being down to 10 men, United prevailed in extra time through a fine shot Norman Whiteside curled round the diving Neville Southall.

Perhaps an incident in an earlier Final had contributed to Moran's dismissal. In 1980, with West Ham leading Arsenal, the 17-year-old Paul Allen broke clear and might have added to Brooking's header but for the cynical challenge from behind by Willie Young that sent him to the turf. The laws of the game at that time did not clearly demand that Young be dismissed, but it was widespread outrage at the injustice of it that led to change. The so-called 'professional foul' was outlawed and, ever since, the last defender has been obliged to think twice about denying a clear goal-scoring opportunity.

The 1987 Final was one long breath of fresh air. Both managers liked to see passing football: David Pleat of Tottenham had even created a five-man midfield in order to liberate the talents of Ossie Ardiles, Chris Waddle and Glenn Hoddle and such was their creativity that the lone striker, Clive Allen, was to end the season with 49 goals. But not a trophy, because the day went to Coventry and their affable boss, John Sillett. The match was wonderfully open and Spurs led 2–1 when Coventry broke and David Bennett, who had put them in front, whipped in a superb cross at which the striker Keith Houchen spectacularly threw himself to head home. In extra time, Spurs' Gary Mabbutt was unkindly awarded an own-goal and Coventry had their first FA Cup success.

A year later it was Wimbledon who did it. Even more remarkably in the sense that the club (later to be controversially moved 60 miles up the M1 and renamed the Milton Keynes Dons) had been elected to membership of the Fourth Division only 11 years earlier. Despite their rise to the top flight playing a vigorous and in many eyes over-aggressive version of the long-ball game, Wimbledon were not expected greatly to trouble an outstanding Liverpool, who were looking to complete the Double. But Lawrie Sanchez headed the underdogs in front and the afternoon's other hero was their goalkeeper, Dave Beasant, who dived his full and considerable length to save a penalty from John Aldridge, the Republic of Ireland striker thereby acquiring the unwanted distinction of being the first man to fail from the spot in an FA Cup Final at Wembley.

When it came to groundbreaking at Wembley, however, the League Cup could more than rival its elder brother. After starting as a two-legged affair, it came to Wembley in 1967 and straight away provided gripping fare. Queens Park Rangers of the Third Division faced West Bromwich Albion of the First. Unfancied QPR were making their first Wembley appearance and initially matters went as expected, the former QPR winger Clive Clark scoring twice for the hot favourites. Then romance took a hand. After Roger Morgan had reduced the deficit with a header, the dashing Rodney Marsh embarked on a sinuous run, tricking several challengers and shooting in off a post. Mark Lazarus hit a late winner. And the magic of this Cup clearly lingered on, for two years later another upwardly mobile Third Division club came and unveiled a giant-slaying hero for the nation to acclaim.

For QPR read Swindon Town. And for Rodney Marsh read Don Rogers. The upstarts were, like QPR before them, to be promoted at the culmination of that season and they showed no lack of ambition on the big occasion, even though they were pitted against Arsenal, whose Bobby Gould cancelled out Roger Smart's opening goal a few minutes from the end of normal time. In extra time, however, Rogers demonstrated that his talent as a goal-scoring winger could move up a level or two with one in each period of extra time, the latter after a run from the halfway line.

Then there was the League Cup Final of 1988, when once again Arsenal were the victims, this time of the team from the same division, although Luton Town were below them in the table (Arsenal finished sixth, Luton ninth). By now the League Cup was bearing the names of its successive sponsors and was known as the Littlewoods Challenge Cup. Before this it had been the Milk Cup and later it was to acknowledge the beneficence of Rumbelows, Coca-Cola, Worthington and Carling. Luton claimed their first-ever honour in an exciting match, Brian Stein's second goal of the afternoon giving the Bedfordshire club victory in the last minute. A measure of their achievement is that Arsenal were not only the Cup holders but were building so impressively under George Graham that they would conclude the following season as champions, clinching the title at Liverpool in extraordinary circumstances as Michael Thomas snatched glory from the hands of the home side in the 94th minute.

What emotional weeks they were as the season of 1988-1989 drew to its unforgettable close. The FA Cup Final was to be perhaps the most emotional of all: inevitable in the year of Hillsborough. Liverpool, having won their Semi-Final against Nottingham Forest when it was completed a few weeks after the disaster had befallen their supporters, met Everton, Merseyside uniting in both grief and the need for some kind of catharsis. John Aldridge put Liverpool ahead but the Everton substitute Stuart McCall equalised to send the match into extra time. The stage was set for the great Ian Rush

RADIO TIMES
FULL BBC SOUND AND TELEVISION PROGRAMMES
ENGLAND
SCOTLAND

to come on and score twice, which meant that another defiant reply from McCall was inadequate to deny Kenny Dalglish's reds. The Wembley fences had been removed as a mark of respect to those who had died behind the barriers at Hillsborough and at the final whistle there was a pitch invasion: inappropriate and mercifully limited to a few spectators.

Because of Lord Taylor's inquiry into Hillsborough, England's leading football stadiums became all-seater, including Wembley, whose capacity was initially reduced to 80,000. In 1990 Alex Ferguson's Manchester United made their breakthrough in the FA Cup. Crystal Palace, making their Wembley debut, gave them quite a match and went 3–2 up in extra-time through Ian Wright, who had been only a substitute because he lacked full fitness. But Mark Hughes equalised and the replay was decided by a goal from the full-back Lee Martin. For United, many more trophies were to follow, but Ferguson has never forgotten that early in that campaign, before Hughes slanted the ball in for Mark Robins to score a momentous winner at Nottingham Forest, even he was questioning his ability to restore United to the status they had occupied at the peak of the Busby era.

In 1991 Tottenham beat Nottingham Forest 2–1 after extra time without the assistance of Paul Gascoigne, who had injured himself in wildly challenging Gary Charles early in the match (after thwarting Arsenal in the Semi-Final, held at Wembley, with a magnificent goal from a free-kick). But Chelsea were to become more frequent visitors, losing 4–0 to United under Glenn Hoddle in 1994, beating Middlesbrough 2–0 under Ruud Gullit in 1997 and finally overcoming Aston Villa 1–0 under Gianluca Vialli a few months before the stadium closed in 2000.

Newcastle United, who had made themselves almost synonymous with the FA Cup by winning it three times between 1951 and 1955, bade farewell to the doomed twin towers with a whimper. Or two whimpers. Miserably they lost 2–0 to Arsenal in 1998 and a year later they were little more than bit-players in the second part of Manchester United's Treble, again losing 2–0.

And so it was left to Chelsea and Villa to play the concluding FA Cup Final under the towers. It may have been a new millennium, but it was the old story of a match that failed to live up to expectations. A goal from Roberto Di Matteo, who had scored spectacularly in the first minute of the 1997 Final, did the trick after David James had weakly punched out a free-kick by Gianfranco Zola. Although the goalkeeper was criticised for not trying to catch the ball, Zola's had been a wicked delivery. The issue was debatable.

Ever since 1923 and West Ham's pleas for the match to be called off because of the crowds on the pitch, there had been points of contention. On this occasion, there was even controversy about the celebrations, because the Chelsea captain, Dennis Wise, chose to collect the trophy with his baby son Henry in his arms. Some thought this a pleasant reflection of the changed nature of male parenthood. Others considered it exhibitionism. We shall never know what the towers thought; their faces, turned down Wembley Way, were silent as ever.

The Auld Enemy

The oldest international fixture in the world had been played for 52 years, interrupted only by the First World War, before Wembley encountered it in April 1924, a year after the stadium's opening. England and Scotland drew 1–1 in front of fewer than 40,000 spectators. When England next played host to the Scots in 1926, it was in Manchester – Wembley was busy with the British Empire Exhibition – but the Auld Enemy soon returned on a regular basis and made their mark with emphasis. It was 1928, the year of the Wembley Wizards, when the Scots came south and inflicted England's heaviest home defeat: by a margin of four goals, one more than was to be the case when the Hungarians visited in 1953. Not even in Glasgow's most partisan quarter had it been remotely expected. The Scottish press had been almost scathing about a selection that pitted, for example, Tom Bradshaw, an international debutant from Bury, at centre-half, where he would have to mark the great Dixie Dean.

Scotland's five forwards were all on the small side; at 5ft 7in, Alec Jackson was the tallest. Yet this was to emerge as a virtue and the captain, Jimmy McMullan, may have discerned it in advance for, when asked to give a tactical talk in the team's hotel the night before the match, he simply advised his colleagues: 'Go to bed and pray for rain'. The torrent duly arrived and a slippery pitch suited the more nimble Scots, who led 2–0 at the interval and improved thereafter, utterly controlling events with prolonged passing movements that verged on the impudent at times. They won 5–1, a hat-trick coming from Jackson, and England's goal was no more than a late gesture. The critics north of the border overlooked their scepticism as the triumph was hailed as a vindication of the Scottish style, a victory for skill over power.

For more than a century, until the early 1980s, the Scots led in the series – the inevitable highlight of the Home International

Opposite — The Royal Flag of Scotland is held aloft by Scottish fans crowded into Wembley Stadium for an England versus Scotland match, 1957.

Championship, which also involved Wales and Northern Ireland – in terms of matches won. But they took some fearful poundings at Wembley, which became known as the graveyard of their goalkeepers' reputations. Fred Martin of Aberdeen had already featured in a massive loss – 7–0 by Uruguay – when he was on the wrong end of a 7–2 defeat by England in 1955 in which Wolves' Dennis Wilshaw scored four. Martin never represented his country again. In 1961 the hapless Frank Haffey from Celtic suffered for a 9–3 thrashing and an abiding memory of 1975, when England won 5–1, is of Rangers' Stewart Kennedy clinging helplessly to a goalpost as the ball swirled around the net.

There were happier moments for the Scots: notably in 1967, when they could claim to be unofficial world champions. And in front of their own fans, who by now were travelling in vast numbers, often to be in the majority at a packed Wembley.

The official world champions, of course, were England, who had gone 19 matches unbeaten (including the historic Final against West Germany) when Scotland came in April 1967. Alf Ramsey's team featured just one change from the historic final: Jimmy Greaves for Roger Hunt. Most Scots felt that it only made the enemy stronger. England were odds-on favourites to beat a team under the new management of Bobby Brown and lacking the tricky winger Jimmy Johnstone, who had scored twice against the English in Glasgow the last time the countries had met. But other factors came into play, notably the resentment of certain Scots, who were tired of the boasting of the Englishmen with whom they shared dressing-rooms.

Denis Law is a good example. There was the well-known and entirely credible tale of how Law, upon coming off a Manchester golf course on the afternoon England won the World Cup, had been informed of the result by a jubilant Englishman. 'Bastards,' muttered Law, who had just lost to his golfing partner and been obliged to hand over £10. 'That makes my day.' Now at Wembley there was an opportunity for him to spoil England's day. Law and Jim Baxter, who had left Rangers for Sunderland and remained just fit enough to give a reprise of his greatness, were to enjoy themselves hugely. At one stage of a 3–2 victory – it could have been more, given the effect on England of an injury that meant Jack Charlton could scarcely run, but some Scots preferred to tease their opponents – Baxter was said to have glanced at Law's Manchester United club mate Stiles, a little man not normally to be trifled with. 'Who are you, son?' he asked. 'Jimmy Clitheroe?'

After Law and Bobby Lennox had given Scotland a two-goal lead, Jack Charlton, bravely serving the English cause as best he could up front, reduced the leeway but the debutant Jim McCalliog made it 3–1 and Geoff Hurst completed the scoring. Many of the 30,000 Scots on the slopes invaded the pitch and embraced their heroes.

In 1977 it happened again and, for some of the hosts, the Scots' visit was marred both by the result – goals from Gordon McQueen and Kenny Dalglish gave Scotland a 2–1 win – and the excesses of the scenes afterwards as thousands took to the turf, tearing it up for souvenirs, dancing in the goalmouths and swinging on the crossbars, one of which snapped under their weight.

The party, though, was all but over. Of the 13 further matches played before the series as such was abandoned in 1988, amid concerns about hooliganism and a view that both countries should look farther afield, Scotland were to win only two. They returned to Wembley in 1996 for the European Championship, in which they were drawn in the hosts' group, losing to goals by Alan Shearer and Paul Gascoigne, the latter memorable for the craft with which Gazza flicked the ball over Colin Hendry before sweeping it home. Things might have been closer but for Gary McAllister letting David Seaman stop a penalty at a crucial stage.

Once more the countries were drawn together in the 1999 play-offs for a place in the following summer's European Championship and, after Paul Scholes had appeared to settle matters with two goals in Glasgow to which the Scots had no answer, the second leg at Wembley a few days later ended nail-bitingly after Don Hutchinson had pulled one back. By now the Scotland fans were less boisterous than the previous generation. Indeed they had a worldwide reputation for losing with good cheer. As, gathered at the old Wembley for the last time, they watched their team fail valiantly, they sang one of their favourite songs: 'Doe, a deer, a female deer ...' Where once there had been the sound of fury, there was 'The Sound of Music'.

England against the World

It has been called the most significant match ever played on an English football field. It is certainly one that lives in Wembley's memory, because England had never lost a home international to visitors from overseas until the dark November day in 1953 when Hungary came and won 6–3.

Most of England's internationals had hitherto taken place on tour or at club grounds such as Highbury, where the Hungarians had lost 6–2 in 1936 as the war clouds gathered. Wembley began to be used by the national team only in the early 1950s, Austria

01

02

03

04

'The three goals that broke England's heart' – England versus Hungary, 1953. In a nine-minute spell, the legendary Wembley Wizards ended England's hopes as Hungary easily won the match 6-3.

01 The English and Hungarian captains, Ferenc Puskás (left) and Billy Wright lead their teams out on to Wembley's famous pitch, 1953.

02 Hungary's third goal is scored by the team captain Ferenc Puskás (number 10).

03 English goalkeeper Gil Merrick fails to save a second goal by Hungary. England's left-back, Bill Eckersley (left), stands next to the fallen Merrick.

04 Hungarian centre-forward Nándor Hidegkuti scores his team's sixth and final goal.

achieving the most promising result, a 2–2 draw. Only the most discerning coaches and critics could discern the revolution that was to come. In a mere 90 minutes, the Magical Magyars, as the Hungarians were dubbed by sections of an admiring press, ensured that England would never again be able to rely on its divine right as football's birthplace.

The lesson began after less than 60 seconds, when the Hungarians burst through the middle and Nándor Hidegkuti, having feinted and sidestepped Harry Johnston, lashed the ball past Gilbert Merrick. Hidegkuti, whose roamings from a notional station as a deep-lying centre-forward confused England, was denied by an offside decision after a beautiful move before Jackie Sewell hit back. Equality, however, was an illusion. Before the half-hour mark the Hungarians led 4–1 through Hidegkuti from close range and two from the great Ferenc Puskás, the first a classic, fizzed high into the net with his lethal left foot at Merrick's near post after a dragback had left Billy Wright, the England captain, on his bottom. Bravely Stanley Matthews and Stanley Mortensen tried to haul England back into contention, Mortensen scoring before the interval. József Bozsik struck with a rising drive and Hidegkuti completed his hat-trick in style, volleying home a Puskás lob, before Alf Ramsey converted a late penalty.

There were 100,000 in the stadium to see this technical and tactical masterclass, which was amply chronicled by, among others, the distinguished football journalist Geoffrey Green. 'There is no sense in writing that England were a poor side,' he told his readers in *The Times*. 'Everything in this world is comparative. Taken within the framework of British football they were acceptable.' The same team, he felt – with the addition of Tom Finney, who missed the Hungary match – could probably beat Scotland, the traditional benchmark, at Hampden Park next April (England were indeed to win 4–2 in Glasgow). 'But here, on Wembley's velvet turf, they found themselves strangers in a strange world, a world of flitting red spirits, for such did the Hungarians seem as they moved at devastating pace with superb skill and powerful finish in their cherry bright shirts.'

Green is worth quoting at greater length: 'One has talked about the new conception of football as developed by the continentals and South Americans. Always the main criticism against the style has been its lack of a final punch near goal. One has thought at times, too, that perhaps the perfection of football was to be found somewhere between the hard hitting, open British method and this other, more subtle, probing infiltration.

'Yesterday the Hungarians, with perfect team work, demonstrated this midway point to perfection. Theirs was a mixture of exquisite short passing and the long English game. The whole of it was knit by exact ball control and mounted by a speed of movement and surprise of thought that had an English team ground into Wembley's pitch a long way from the end. The Hungarians, in fact, moved the ball swiftly along the ground with delicate flicks or used the long pass in the air. And the point was that they used these variations as they wished, changing the point of attack at remarkable speed. To round it off – this was the real point – they shot with the accuracy and speed of archers. It was Agincourt in reverse.'

The following year England went to Budapest and lost 7–1. They could no longer claim to be the dominant force in football: far from it, but among those taking the lesson to heart, after receiving it on the pitch, was Alf Ramsey. When Ramsey, having gone into management and won the championship at Ipswich Town, took over the national squad in 1963, he was the first to have complete control of the team. The only previous manager, Walter Winterbottom, had been subject to the FA's selection committee, although they usually sought his advice.

It was some years after the shock delivered by the Hungarians that he produced one of his finest sides. Between October 1960 and May 1961 they won six consecutive matches, scoring no fewer than forty goals – Jimmy Greaves got eleven, Bobby Charlton and the burly Bobby Smith eight each – and conceding eight. The last four were at Wembley. First Spain, their reputation sky-high because Real Madrid had been ruling European club football since its inception, were beaten 4–2 with Smith prominent. Then Wales lost 5–1 and Scotland 9–3 (with Bobby Robson among those who found the net) before Mexico were routed 8–0. England's earlier victims had been Northern Ireland in Belfast and Luxembourg in the Grand Duchy.

Greaves, Charlton and Smith apart, England's creative influences included the winger Bryan Douglas and midfielder Johnny Haynes, arguably as elegant and penetrative a passer as the country has ever produced. They went to the World Cup in Chile in 1962 but proved no match for Brazil, who knocked them out in the Quarter-Finals.

A few months later Ramsey took charge and, retaining Bobby Charlton and Greaves, began the long process of trial and error that was to lead to glory. Among his key decisions were the appointment of Bobby Moore as captain and the introduction of Roger Hunt and, later, Geoff Hurst and the young Alan Ball.

Opposite — Bobby Charlton and the Benfica captain, Mário Coluna, exchange pennants before the European Cup Final, 1968. Manchester United beat Benfica 4–1.

CAPITÃO
MANCHESTER UNITED
FOOTBALL CLUB
DO
SPORT LISBOA e BENFICA
AO
MANCHESTER UNITED
FINAL
LONDRES
29-5-968

01

02

03

04

05

01 A Merseyside derby at Wembley. Team captains Kevin Ratcliffe (left) of Everton and Ronnie Whelan (right) of Liverpool shake hands before the FA Cup Final, 1989.

02 Ian Rush of Liverpool scores the second goal in the derby final, helping his team to a 3–2 victory.

03 Following a pulsating 3–3 draw in the FA Cup Final, Manchester United's Lee Martin scores the winning goal in a crowded Crystal Palace penalty area in the replay at Wembley, 1990. Manchester United defeated Crystal Palace 1–0.

04 The victorious Manchester United team celebrate with the trophy.

05 Alex Ferguson, manager of Manchester United, raises the FA Cup, 1990.

A run of seven victories took England to the opening match of the 1966 tournament, in which they met Uruguay and looked unimaginative during a scoreless draw. They were scarcely more exciting in beating Mexico and France, each by 2–0. After the France match, in which the tackling of Nobby Stiles had been considered too rough, the FA told Ramsey to drop the Manchester United midfielder and, predictably, he refused. So England, having won their group and thereby ensured they would stay at Wembley for as long as they remained in the tournament, prepared to meet Argentina with their gap-toothed destroyer.

The Argentines had clearly resolved to meet Stiles with fire of their own and, after the German referee had taken a few of their names, the captain, Antonio Rattín, protested so vehemently that he was sent off. For eight minutes he refused to leave the field but the match resumed and Hurst, with a header, won it.

Now Wembley was richly entertained, for the ensuing Semi-Final, against Portugal, was superb. Bobby Charlton got both of England's goals, the latter was one of those spectacular long-range drives for which he became famous, and the great Eusébio replied with a penalty, Gordon Banks being beaten for the first time in the tournament. And the drama became almost relentless as the old stadium hosted its momentous Final.

West Germany took the lead through Helmut Haller and nerves may have played a part, for the normally reliable left-back, Ray Wilson, had headed the ball straight to Haller. Before long Hurst's head skilfully guided Moore's free-kick past Hans Tilkowski and 12 minutes from the scheduled end England took the lead through Martin Peters. England appeared hard done by at the eleventh hour when, Jack Charlton and Sigi Held having collided in the air, the Germans were given the free-kick, from which Wolfgang Weber equalised, but they certainly got the rub of the green when the Hurst shot was judged by a linesman from Azerbaijan, Tofik Bakhramov, to have crossed the goal-line. The stage was set for Hurst to round off his hat-trick, Kenneth Wolstenholme to emit his deathless lines and the nation, with the notably stone-faced exception of Ramsey, to celebrate with abandon.

Wembley was not to remain an impregnable fortress. There were significant defeats: 3–1 by West Germany in a European Championship qualifier in 1972, when Günther Netzer claimed the stage; 2–0 by Holland in 1977, when Jan Peters scored both goals; and 1–0 by Denmark in 1983 are examples. But the 1980s ended well under Bobby Robson, who introduced Wembley to the delights of Paul Gascoigne in a 4–2 win over Czechoslovakia shortly before the World Cup in Italy, where England reached the Semi-Finals.

Under Graham Taylor they failed to reach the 1994 tournament but to his successor, Terry Venables, fell the honour, privilege and burden of preparing the side for a European Championship held, like the World Cup three decades earlier, on home soil.

Football Comes Home

Seldom can a tournament slogan have become so popular as that of the European Championship of 1996, held in England, which had decided to proclaim its heritage. 'Football Comes Home' was such an apt line that the comedians David Baddiel and Frank Skinner adopted it for the chorus of the England team's official song, *Three Lions*. With the Lightning Seeds providing the music, Baddiel and Skinner wrote in an aspirational rather than triumphalist vein, harking back to World Cup success in 1966 and the various disappointments that had followed:

Three Lions on a shirt
Jules Rimet still gleaming
Thirty years of hurt
Never stopped me dreaming.

And the chorus, which was to resonate all the way to the Semi-Finals, and indeed thereafter, for England's German conquerors took it up with glee, went:

It's coming home
It's coming home
It's coming
Football's coming home.

In fact the England squad, under the management of Terry Venables, had come home for the tournament under something of a cloud. Their preparations had consisted of an apparently interminable succession of home friendlies, three of which were scoreless draws, and then matches in China and Hong Kong. After the latter the players went to a nightclub, where the so-called 'dentist's chair' episode took place. Several players, inevitably including Paul Gascoigne, playfully sat back while strong drinks such as tequila were poured down their throats from a great height. Photographs appeared in the press and there was quite a controversy, to which Gazza was playfully to allude in his celebrations after he had dazzlingly scored against Scotland; he lay back and opened his mouth while team mates squeezed water-bottles from above.

But England's tournament began quietly for, although Alan Shearer, ending a long spell without an international goal, put them ahead after 23 minutes against Switzerland, a late penalty by Kubilay Türkyilmaz denied them victory. They got full points from Scotland thanks to Shearer again and Gazza and then came one of their most vivid displays of modern times; that it was imposed on a poor Dutch side should not detract from its majesty, rounded off by two goals each from the front pair of Shearer (one was a penalty) and Teddy Sheringham. The best, making the score 3–0 after 57 minutes, summed up everything Venables had wanted from his creative influences. Gascoigne, receiving from Darren Anderton, played a one-two with Steve McManaman that got him into the penalty area, where he pulled the ball back for Sheringham, who – and this was the key – first-timed it sideways to Shearer. After the rapier came the bludgeon, with which the centre-forward drove it irresistibly past Edwin van der Sar. For Venables, the joy was enhanced by his long-time admiration for Holland's teams of the past and their tactical excellence; now, at Wembley, he had outmanoeuvred them.

England, having qualified in first place in their group (Holland's consolation goal, put through David Seaman's legs by the substitute Patrick Kluivert, edged out the Scots), stayed at Wembley for the Quarter-Final. It was against Spain, who, orchestrated by Fernando Hierro in midfield, were the better side but suffered from poor decisions by the French referee, Marc Batta, and his linesmen and lost on penalties; after David Seaman had thwarted Hierro, a miss by Miguel Angel Nadal, later to achieve further fame as the uncle of a tennis sensation, sealed the Spaniards' fate.

England were back near their best for the Semi-Final against Germany. They took an early lead when Gascoigne's corner was nodded on at the near post for Shearer to head his fifth goal of the tournament (he finished up its leading scorer) but soon Thomas Helmer crossed for Stefan Kuntz to beat Stuart Pearce to the ball and equalise. In extra time Anderton struck a post and Kuntz again had the ball in the net only to be pulled up for a shove on Adams. The most memorable thrill, though, was provided by Gascoigne's valiant but vain slide at a low cross from Shearer in the 99th minute; under the golden-goal rule, a successful contact would have meant sudden death for the Germans, but Gascoigne was to miss by inches. Again the issue went to penalties and, with the sides tied on 5–5, Gareth Southgate had one saved by Andreas Köpke. As the central defender stood aghast, Venables did not hesitate. For the departing manager – his contract ended with England's campaign – disappointment must have been intense. But he wiped it off his face and bravely smiled as he ran to console Southgate.

In the Final, Germany, now reunited, met the Czech Republic, which had split from Slovakia. It hardly seemed a fair fight but Patrik Berger, with a penalty, had the Czechs in front until Oliver Bierhoff, on just four minutes as a replacement for Mehmet Scholl, took the match into extra time, which had lasted a mere five minutes when Bierhoff struck again, making the Germans the first team to win a major international title on the golden goal (France were to follow in their footsteps in the European Championship of 2000). Berti Vogts was their manager. His masterstroke had been to make Jürgen Klinsmann captain even though he knew he would have to do without Lothar Matthäus; these two stars did not get on. Other heroes were the elegant *libero* Matthias Sammer and the midfield workhorse Dieter Eilts.

Later Klinsmann was to disclose that during the tournament the Germans had developed a liking for the *Three Lions* and even sung it on the way to Wembley for their confrontation with the English. In Germany, amazingly, the Lightning Seeds' single had reached No. 16 in the charts. In England, of course, it reached No. 1. But the Germans had the trophy. *Fussball* was going home.

Kevin Keegan and the Final Curtain

Wembley was to become Gareth Southgate's bogey ground. Not until the place had closed and the Millennium Stadium become the venue of Cup Finals did his luck change: there in Cardiff in 2004, as captain of Steve McClaren's Middlesbrough, he lifted the League Cup after a 2–1 victory over Bolton. But on the fateful afternoon of 7 October 2000, he once again took an inadvertent role in an England downfall. Or was said to have done for, while he neither missed a penalty not committed any other gaffe, Southgate was held by many critics to be centrally involved in the defeat by Germany that got the qualification process for the World Cup of 2002 off to a deceptively awful start and prompted Kevin Keegan's startling resignation as manager.

Throughout Euro '96, Southgate had been a sound partner for Tony Adams in Terry Venables's defence. But now the central pairing was of Arsenal's Adams and Martin Keown, and Keegan, in an attempt to stiffen the resistance further, drafted in Southgate

01

02

03

01 An aerial view of Wembley Stadium in the 1990s.

02 Football comes home. 'Three Lions' enter into the aspirational English spirit of the European Championship, 1996.

03 Balloons are released at Wembley signalling the start of Euro '96. England drew 1–1 with Switzerland in the opening game.

01

02

03

On a sad, bewildering and desperately dramatic evening for English football, Wembley Stadium was led away to the knacker's yard and Kevin Keegan fell upon his sword.
MAIL ON SUNDAY, 8 OCTOBER 2000

01 Bedraggled fans walk along Olympic Way towards the stadium for the England versus Germany match, 9 October 2000. It was the final competitive game played at Wembley before the old stadium closed.

02 Germany's Dietmar 'Didi' Hamann celebrates the last goal scored in the old stadium, 2000.

03 The dejected England coach, Kevin Keegan, walks off the pitch after losing 1–0 to Germany. It was to be his last game as manager; he resigned shortly afterwards.

– who had made his reputation as a midfielder at Crystal Palace before being converted to a centre-back at Aston Villa – to play in front of the back four. It was not Southgate's fault that England were utterly outmanoeuvred in the midfield, where Didi Hamann ruled, ably supported by the burgeoning Michael Ballack. The Germans did play very well. Had Steven Gerrard (England's brightest young hope in those days, before the emergence of Wayne Rooney) been fit and able to take the position, things might not have been radically different. A lot of the scorn that was directed at Southgate for having been picked by the manager was unfair but convenient; disdain might have equally been heaped on Keegan or David Seaman for failing to stop the match-winning-kick.

The day had begun with optimism. True, England had performed poorly under Keegan in the European Championship a few months earlier, letting both Portugal and Romania come from behind to win and being knocked out at the group stage. But their only victory had come against the Germans, whose crisis at the time was clearly more profound, and there was optimism that England would give the twin towers one last experience of triumph over their great rivals.

Not only that: when Keegan awoke at the team's hotel and threw open the curtains, he must have felt like giving a thumbs-up to the leaden sky. With the home side under an obligation to force the pace, a slippery surface provided by rain would help them to get behind German defenders hardly noted for their poise. In the event, however, the weather did too zealous a job and the pitch was heavy, though this did not constrain Rudy Voeller's Germans from giving a display both athletic and accomplished on it. More than anything, they won the tactical contest, as Keegan was to acknowledge in his dramatic resignation afterwards.

The origin of his problems may have lain in a reluctance to see the merits of the 3-5-2 formation with which he had experimented prior to the European Championship. There certainly seemed a need to thicken the midfield after the summer setbacks. Yet, when the team-sheet was handed out to the media less than an hour before kick-off, gasps of dismay greeted the recognition of a basic 4-4-2 with, moreover, two decidedly non-complementary strikers in Michael Owen and Andrew Cole, neither of whom liked to drop off the front. Accordingly they spent most of the afternoon isolated. The central midfielder supposed to be serving them with passes, Paul Scholes, kept moving deep in order to help Southgate to cope with the clever and mobile Mehmet Scholl, while the men on the flanks, David Beckham and Nicky Barmby, were sucked in, leaving wide corridors through which Sebastian Deisler and Marco Bode could attack. Fittingly, the only goal would be scored by the majestic man-of-the-match Hamann, whose free-kick (conceded by Scholes with a foul on Ballack) squeezed past Seaman.

A switch to 3-5-2 for the second half made quite a difference, with Beckham's more central position allowing Scholes to get forward, but the confident Germans survived without too much trouble and Keegan, whose reign had been ushered in a mere twenty months earlier on a great tide of euphoria, had no doubt as to what he must do.

It had always been predicted that he would leave on an impulse – twice he had stalked away from Newcastle United only to be coaxed back – but he hinted that resignation had been on his mind when he disclosed: 'I've probably had a longer run than I expected after Euro 2000. Managers who did better than me have fallen by the wayside.' With typical candour, he added that there was no one to blame but himself, given that the FA had 'backed me all the way' and the players given all they could. There were good youngsters coming through, too, 'but I know I'm not the man to lead them'.

Later it was discovered that Keegan's mother had died only eleven days earlier, and that may have clarified his decision-making process by inducing a sense of perspective. That everything about the England manager's life is liable to be blown out of proportion was illustrated by accusations that he had let his country down. England had to play Finland in Helsinki four days later and there, under the temporary charge of Howard Wilkinson, they dropped another two points, though they were unlucky that a drive from Ray Parlour which bounced down off the crossbar and over the line did not receive the approval accorded Geoff Hurst's effort thirty-four years earlier.

Next Peter Taylor, with the assistance of Steve McClaren, took over for a friendly against Italy in Turin – England lost, but made a significant advance with Taylor's appointment of David Beckham as captain – watched by their next full-time boss, Sven-Göran Eriksson. Under Eriksson the initial improvement was so dramatic that on 1 September 2001, less than eleven months after the humbling by the Germans at Wembley, England won 5–1 in Munich. But Eriksson was never to manage an England team at Wembley. Nor was Beckham to lead them out. Those distinctions were for the standard-bearers of a new era. As the arch rose where the towers had been, the memory of Keegan's sad farewell was buried under a great symbol of optimism.

My horse was wonderful, gently easing folk back with his nose and tail until we had pushed the crowd over one of the goal lines. Billy seemed to understand exactly what was wanted of him.

PC George Scorey, Policeman at the FA Cup Final — 28 April 1923

01

02

03

04

05

Previous page — Mounted police, among them PC George Scorey on his white horse Billy, attempt to clear the pitch before the start of the first FA Cup Final at Wembley, 1923.

01 Crowds at the turnstiles before the FA Cup Final between West Ham United and Bolton Wanderers at Wembley (then known as the Empire Stadium).

02 In excess of 200,000 fans poured into a stadium designed to accommodate 126,500. The massive crowd was forced out of the stands and on to the pitch by sheer weight of numbers.

03 Police officers on horseback and on foot struggle to control the swelling FA Cup Final crowd, 1923.

04 Bolton Wanderers fans are pushed back behind the goalposts.

05 A programme and souvenir for the 1923 FA Cup Final at the Empire Stadium Wembley.

06

07

In Affectionate Remembrance
OF
WEST HAM
WHO WERE
DEFEATED TO-DAY
Boldly to the match they went,
Their hearts, on winning the match were bent;
But with sad hearts they came away,
They found their masters at the play
Twas two good teams that played to-day
But the best team won with great display
Please do not weep No onions required
BETTER LUCK NEXT TIME

08

06–07 Play in the 1923 FA Cup Final finally commenced forty-five minutes late. Bolton Wanderers defeated West Ham United 2–0.

08 This satirical rhyming card was printed and circulated on the very day of the 1923 FA Cup Final, in 'remembrance' of the defeat suffered by West Ham United at the hands of Bolton Wanderers.

I don't even recall any other children or women being there. I just remember grown men wearing hats. The Bolton supporters were wearing flat caps and the West Ham fans had trilbies. DENIS HIGHAM, WHO ATTENDED THE 1923 CUP FINAL, AGED EIGHT, INTERVIEWED IN THE INDEPENDENT, 18 MAY 2007

But here, on Wembley's velvet turf, they found themselves strangers in a strange world, a world of flitting red spirits, for such did the Hungarians seem as they moved at devastating pace with superb skill and powerful finish in their cherry bright shirts.

Geoffrey Green, *The Times* — 26 November 1953

01

02

03

Previous page — England captain Billy Wright (left), and team mate Alf Ramsey, in the net, look on anxiously as goalkeeper Gil Merrick tips a shot round the post during a Hungarian attack at the England goal in the international match at Wembley, 1953. England lost 6–3.

01 Alan Sealey beats the keeper to score West Ham's second goal against TSV Munich in the Final of the European Cup-Winners' Cup, 1965.

02 Alan Sealey scores the first of his two goals in the 1965 European Cup-Winners' Cup Final at Wembley.

03 Geoff Hurst, Martin Peters and the West Ham team hold Bobby Moore aloft with the 1965 Cup-Winners' Cup.

04

05

06

04 Benfica's goalkeeper José Henrique (left) races back to his goal in a vain attempt to stop George Best (right) of Manchester United from scoring his team's second goal in the European Cup Final at Wembley, 1968. United eventually won 4–1 after extra time.

05 Best celebrates his goal, which gave Manchester United the lead.

06 Bobby Charlton, captain of Manchester United, holds aloft the European Cup after his team's victory over Benfica.

01

02

03

04

05

06

07

Opposite — England captain Bobby Moore leads his side out on to the Wembley pitch for the 1966 World Cup Quarter-Final, the beginning of a fiery encounter with the opposing Argentine team.

01 An official tournament poster for the 1966 FIFA World Cup in England, featuring its mascot 'World Cup Willie'.

02 Geoff Hurst jubilant after heading in England's winning goal against Argentina at Wembley Stadium, 1966. England won the game 1–0.

03 Argentina's Silvio Marzolini leaves the field after an ill-tempered match.

04 England manager Alf Ramsey prevents George Cohen from swapping his shirt with an Argentinian player following a bad tempered World Cup Quarter-Final. Afterwards, Ramsey described the Argentinian team as a pack of 'animals'.

05 Police officers escort referee R Kritlin of West Germany off the pitch at the end of the match. His dismissal of Argentine captain, Rattín, was followed by an eight-minute delay as the Argentinians threatened to walk off.

06 England's captain Bobby Moore (right) exchanges pennants with Portugal's captain Coluna before the World Cup Semi-Final at Wembley, 1966.

07 England's Nobby Stiles (number 4) watches as Portugal's Eusébio leaps for a header during the 1966 World Cup Semi-Final. England defeated Portugal 2–1.

01

02

03

04

I was seventeen years old at the time. I recall all of the emotions – singing, cheering and then crying at the final. Now forty years later, I regret one thing – not retaining a ticket stub or a programme. GRAHAM WILLSHER, ENGLAND SUPPORTER

01 West Germany's Wolfgang Weber and England's Martin Peters both jump for the ball during the World Cup Final at Wembley, 1966.

02 A sought-after ticket for the 1966 World Cup Final.

03 The cover of the official Wembley 1966 World Cup Final programme, 30 July 1966.

04 Weber scores a dramatic goal in the dying seconds of the game to take the World Cup Final into extra time.

05

06

07

05 Geoff Hurst scores the third goal of the World Cup Final, 1966. The Russian linesman famously gave the goal allowing England to go on to win 4–2 in extra time.

06 English players celebrate as referee Gottfried Dienst gives the controversial Hurst goal after consulting the linesman.

07 Champions of the World! Geoff Hurst is ecstatic after his third goal.

Overleaf — English football's greatest moment. England team members mount Wembley's famous thirty-nine steps to collect the trophy from Her Majesty the Queen, following their 4–2 win against West Germany in the World Cup Final, 1966.

ENGLAND v GERMANY — 1966
World Cup Final

Any second now, it will all be over.
Thirty seconds by our watch,
and the Germans are going down
and they can hardly get up.
It's all over I think.
No, it's …
And here comes Hurst, he's got …
Some people are on the pitch
they think it's all over
IT IS NOW … IT'S FOUR!

Kenneth Wolstenholme, BBC Commentator — 30 July 1966

01

02

03

04

05

06

01 Members of Chelsea and Leeds United hobble off the Wembley pitch after their 2–2 draw in a brutal FA Cup Final, 1970. The replay was held at Old Trafford, Manchester with Chelsea winning 2–1.

02 Arsenal's Charlie George scores the winning goal against Liverpool to seal the win 2–1 in the 1971 FA Cup Final and clinch the coveted Double.

03 Sunderland manager Bob Stokoe celebrates his team's victory over Leeds United in the 1973 FA Cup Final, one of the greatest Wembley wins by an underdog.

04 Sunderland's Ian Porterfield is mobbed by team mates after scoring the only goal of the 1973 FA Cup Final.

05 West Ham United striker Alan Taylor raises his arms in glee after scoring one of his two match-winning goals in The FA Cup Final, 1975.

06 Bobby Moore bids farewell to Wembley after Fulham's 2–0 defeat to West Ham in the 1975 Final. Moore consoles former team mate Billy Bonds: 'At our age we shouldn't be playing in a Cup Final. Enjoy it while you can.'

07

08

09

10

11

12

07 The jubilant Southampton team celebrate with the trophy after their 1–0 victory over Manchester United in the FA Cup Final at Wembley, 1976.

08 The luck of the Irish. Arsenal fans cheer on their strong Irish contingent at the 1978 FA Cup Final.

09 The 'Five Minute Final' of 1979. Arsenal's Alan Sunderland scores the dramatic winning goal past Manchester United goalkeeper Gary Bailey, just moments after United had equalised.

10 Arsenal goalkeeper Pat Jennings dives acrobatically across his goal to make a spectacular save from Ipswich Town's George Burley (left) as Paul Mariner looks on in the 1978 FA Cup Final.

11 Arsenal captain Pat Rice raises the FA Cup after beating Manchester United 3–2 in the FA Cup Final, 1979.

12 Ipswich Town's captain Mick Mills parades the FA Cup trophy after winning 1–0 against Arsenal, 1978.

CONGRATULATIONS LIVERPOOL
OF THE EUROPEAN CUP
HARD LUCK

Opposite — Liverpool players carry the trophy on a lap of honour after their 1–0 victory over FC Bruges in the European Cup Final at Wembley, 1978.

Above — Kenny Dalglish of Liverpool watches apprehensively after chipping the ball past FC Bruges goalkeeper Birger Jensen in the 1978 European Cup Final.

Overleaf — Keith Houchen of Coventry City scores a dramatic diving header during the 3–2 FA Cup Final victory over Tottenham Hotspur at Wembley, 1987.

hummel
JR EVENTS

hummel
WEMBLEY
HOSPITALITY PACKAGES
01-902 8833
WEMBLEY TOURS
01-903
4864
NIKE
SOCCER

01

02

03

04

05

01 The Manchester City and Tottenham Hotspur teams are led out on to the Wembley field by their managers – John Bond and Keith Burkinshaw – for the 100th FA Cup Final Replay, 1981.

02 Tottenham's Ricky Villa scores the first of his two goals.

03 Villa goes past City's Ray Ranson on his mazy run for the third goal of the 1981 Final Replay.

04 Ricky Villa slots the ball home to score the final goal, beating Manchester City 3–2.

05 Villa celebrates his team's win, holding aloft the FA Cup trophy.

06

07

08

06 Keeper Dave Beasant denies John Aldridge's penalty, the first penalty save in an FA Cup Final.

07 Liverpool's goalkeeper Bruce Grobbelaar looks dejectedly at the ball in the back of his net after Wimbledon's Lawrie Sanchez scored the only goal of the game with a header.

08 Wimbledon, the 1988 FA Cup Final winners. 'The Crazy Gang' celebrate with the trophy.

01

02

01 'Its Coming Home!' Gazza volleys home England's fantastic winning goal against Scotland in the 1996 European Championship.

02 Gary McAllister of Scotland despairs as he misses a penalty during a Euro '96 match against England at Wembley. England won 2–0.

03

04

05

03 Dutch striker, Patrick Kluivert's late consolation goal eliminates Scotland from the tournament on goal difference during the '96 European Championships.

04 Alan Shearer celebrates his second goal in England's demolition of the Dutch. It is widely considered England's finest performance since 1966.

05 Redemption: England finally win a penalty shoot-out as David Seaman saves an attempt from Spaniard Nadal during Euro '96.

01

02

03

04

05

06

01 The English and German teams line up for their national anthems announcing the Semi-Final of Euro '96.

02 Alan Shearer celebrates his goal against Germany.

03 Germany's Kuntz equalises in the fifteenth minute.

04 Gazza narrowly fails to convert with a cross in the German penalty area.

05 England's miserable penalty shoot-out form returns. Andreas Möller scores the winning penalty in the Semi-Final against old foe, Germany.

06 David Seaman consoles team mate Gareth Southgate after he misses the penalty that put England out of the championship.

Opposite — Southgate despairs following his miss in the penalty shoot-out.

SOUTHGATE
6

01

02

03

01 Gazza (number 8) scores Tottenham Hotspur's first goal of the 1991 FA Cup Semi-Final from a direct free kick.

02 Gazza celebrates his stunning 35-yard goal during the 1991 FA Cup Semi-Final which saw Tottenham Hotspur win 3–1 against local rivals, Arsenal.

03 Gazza receives treatment after injuring himself while challenging Gary Charles of Nottingham Forest. The injury put Gazza out of football for a year.

04

05

06

07

04 Roberto Di Matteo of Chelsea scores the fastest ever goal at Wembley in a FA Cup Final after just forty-two seconds, 1997.

05 Roberto Di Matteo, Eddie Newton and Dennis Wise of Chelsea celebrate their team's 2–0 victory over Middlesbrough in the 1997 Final.

06 The Chelsea team celebrates its 1–0 win over Aston Villa at the 2000 FA Cup Final, the last to be played at old Wembley.

07 Di Matteo returns. His seventy-second minute winner for Chelsea denied Aston Villa their first Cup triumph since 1957.

01

02

03

04

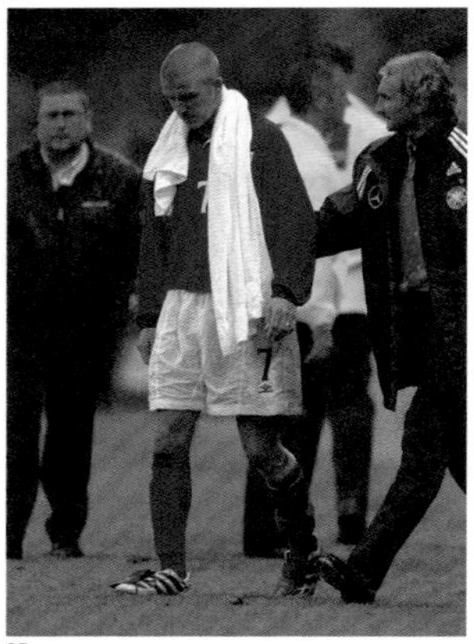

05

It should have been so much better ... for me Wembley has always been a mixture of stunning aura and noxious aroma. At this stadium, I have enjoyed the sight of the great ones in their pomp; Englishmen with names like Matthews, Finney, Edwards and Moore and magnificent foreign performers in Platini, Maradona, Eusébio ...
PATRICK COLLINS, MAIL ON SUNDAY, 8 OCTOBER 2000

01 English and German fans walk up Olympic Way to the old stadium for the last time.

02 Didi Hamann scores the only goal with a quickly taken free kick in the fifteenth minute.

03 English goalkeeper, David Seaman only gets one hand to the ball and fails to stop the shot as captain, Tony Adams looks on. The match was Adams' sixtieth match at Wembley for club and country; the highest number of appearances on the hallowed pitch by any player.

04 Fireworks fizzle over a rain-drenched Wembley; the match followed in a similarly dismal fashion.

05 Dejected, David Beckham trudges off the pitch, consoled by German manager, Rudi Voeller.

Opposite — Goodbye twin towers. Germany, Wembley's most successful foreign team, inflict a final 1–0 defeat on England at the old stadium in a World Cup qualifier, 2000.

Coca-Cola
TIME:90
FIFA 2002 WORLD CUP QUAL'
ENGLAND 0
GERMANY 1
Nationwide

A NEW NATIONAL STADIUM

Kenneth Powell

Describing the new Wembley Stadium its architect, Norman Foster, says: 'the old Wembley was the most famous sports and entertainment venue in Britain – the challenge in reinventing it was to build on that heritage and yet create a venue that would be memorable and magical in its own right'. That, in a nutshell, was the Wembley mission. However, achieving it would not be so straightforward.

Wembley's designation, just before Christmas 1996, as the site of the English National Stadium marked the beginning of the new Wembley Stadium. Fundamental to the project was the transfer of freehold of the old stadium from Wembley plc to a non-profit organisation, the English National Stadium Trust, which could benefit from National Lottery funding. Nobody had a clear idea of what the new stadium would cost to build, but it seemed highly unlikely that the entire cost would be found from Lottery funds, managed by Sport England. Furthermore, a grant of around £100 million to buy the freehold to the stadium site would probably be as much as could be expected and even the most optimistic observer knew that the new stadium could cost three times that amount.

It's worth fast-forwarding at this point to note in fact that the final cost of the building (the hardware as Foster himself likes to call it) was £352 million. In terms of cost per seat, that equates to approximately £3,600 per place, which compares favourably with recent European stadiums that offer nothing like the range of facilities provided at Wembley. The only element of the project that was actually paid for with Lottery money was the land on which the stadium stands. The rest was funded by private investors, including the FA, together with enabling funding from the Department of Culture Media and Sport (DCMS) and the London Development Agency (LDA).

If nobody in the beginning knew how much the new Wembley would cost, there was equal uncertainty about how it should be used. From the beginning there was strong political interest in the project. Following the general election in 1997 the Labour government had created a new ministry, the Department of Culture, Media and Sport, with Tony Banks as minister with responsibility for sport under Secretary of State Chris Smith. Both were London MPs and Banks was a former member of the Greater London Council. The stadium was potentially a popular project which might reflect well on the government and there was also the possibility it could be used for a British bid for the 2006 World Cup or even a future Olympics. Banks declared that 'Wembley is a project that we simply cannot afford to let go wrong'.

The Sports Council (later Sport England), which had the gift of Lottery funds, therefore stipulated that bids for the National Stadium should provide for a wide spectrum of major sporting events, including not only football, but also Rugby League matches (Rugby League had a long and honourable tradition at the old stadium, dating back to 1929) and more significantly athletics track and field events.

These were not the only hurdles the project had to overcome. The old stadium, though much altered since its completion and increasingly seen as shabby and inadequate, was a Grade II listed building: there would have to be very good arguments for its demolition. The expectation was that, at the very least, the facade and 'twin towers' – a truly international 'signature' as English Heritage described them – would have to be retained. (One fulsome account described the towers as presenting 'an omnipresent majesty, somehow comparable to the Swiss side of the Matterhorn as seen from Zermatt'!) There was also the issue of how the other facilities at Wembley, including the Arena and Conference Centre, would relate to the new stadium and what other development might be considered for the former Empire Exhibition site. It was clear that a masterplan was required.

The first work on a stadium masterplan was carried out in the early 1990s. It included plans for rebuilding the stadium whilst retaining the towers. However, the study led nowhere. Foster + Partners first became involved towards the end of 1995. The practice had recently helped to develop the Manchester Olympic bid and was ready to put its expertise to work at Wembley. Foster's masterplan envisaged a brand new stadium – it was obvious that refurbishing the old stadium was not a sensible use of resources – and the creation of new public space around it was a basic ingredient of the plan. 'The scheme was less about the internal workings of a stadium and more about what a stadium gives to the surrounding city', says Foster.

Another factor that helped form the Foster team's vision of a new stadium was the changing nature of big sports venues at that time. Big American stadiums were becoming 365-day-a-year places, and with a renewed interest in sports venues such as Coors Field in Denver or Baltimore's Camden Yards, were viewed increasingly as centres of urban regeneration and renewal. The old Wembley Stadium was profitable, but this was largely due to core FA events being held there each year. When there was no match or other event, it lay idle: a new approach was required.

The Football Association was the key event owner at Wembley, because without the FA there was no viable business plan. (The FA is committed to staging the FA Cup Final and international matches in the new stadium for at least 25 years.) It followed that Ken Bates, as chairman of the FA Board, would have a key role in the development of the project. Bates had taken over Chelsea FC, then debt-ridden and in the Second Division, in 1982. Under his chairmanship Chelsea rose to the Premier League and succeeded in acquiring the freehold of the Stamford Bridge ground, which had been threatened with redevelopment. He led the ambitious project to develop the area around the ground as Chelsea Village, thereby securing the club financially.

Bates regarded the proposed deal with the English National Stadium Trust as fundamentally flawed – it simply perpetuated a system in which Wembley plc creamed off most of the profits of big games. He threatened to walk out of the deal, taking the big football games to venues around Britain and boycotting Wembley altogether. Without football, Bates argued, Wembley could not survive. Bates took a prominent part in the Lottery grant negotiations with the Sports Council. As a result, it was finally agreed that £120 million of Lottery funding should go to a subsidiary of the FA, the English National Stadium Development Company (which later became Wembley National Stadium Ltd) to run the project. Bob Heaver, former chief executive of the English National Stadium Trust (ENST), and Bob Stubbs, who subsequently became chief executive of Wembley National Stadium Ltd (WNSL), also played key roles in these early negotiations.

On 15 March 1999, the English National Stadium Development Company (ENSDC) took formal possession of the stadium and 24 acres of adjacent land, the purchase price being £106 million, which included £3 million in stamp duty and fees. The remaining land around the stadium, including the Wembley Arena and large areas of car parking, was on offer for around £25 million more but the FA declined to bid for it, a decision that Bob Stubbs felt was short-sighted. 'It would have allowed us to build the new stadium anywhere we wanted on the site, allowing us to keep the old one up and running and making money while the new one was built', he argues. It was certainly a decision with significant consequences for the setting of the new stadium and for its future use. The Olympics lobby had pointed out that, if Wembley became a venue for a future Olympiad, extra land would be needed around the stadium, including provision for a warm-up track for athletes. (In fact, a potential location for a warm-up track also existed – and still exists – in the shape of a public park, just across the Chiltern Railway line, immediately to the south of the stadium.)

Once the ENSDC had been established, the process of appointing a professional design team began, following public procurement rules. It was at this point that Foster + Partners teamed up with the sports division of HOK, the leading practice in American stadium design, and the LOBB Partnership, responsible for the Millennium Stadium in Cardiff and Stadium Australia (built for the 2000 Olympics in Sydney) as well as the Matthew Harding Stand at Stamford Bridge for Chelsea. (During 1998 HOK and LOBB came together under the HOK Sport banner and the practice is now known as HOK Sport + Venue + Event.) At Norman Foster's suggestion the combined Foster + Partners, HOK and LOBB teams called themselves the World Stadium Team. It was a formidable and, as it turned out, unbeatable alliance.

In May 1998 the World Stadium Team was named as the winner of the architectural bid to be designers of the new stadium, beating two other short-listed practices. From Foster + Partners the team at this point comprised Norman Foster, Ken Shuttleworth and Huw Thomas, with Alistair Lenczner (who had been recruited from Arup, where he'd worked on the Bari stadium project for the Italia '90 World Cup) and Angus Campbell who, with Lenczner, would see the project through to completion. (Mouzhan Majidi, now Chief Executive of Foster + Partners, who was later to take a leading role in the project, was then still in Hong Kong, completing the Chek Lap Kok airport project.) On the HOK side, Ben Vickery (who had worked on the Chelsea stand with LOBB) returned to London from Australia to work on the scheme: 'it was a genuine collaboration all the way through', he recalls; and David Manica of HOK's Kansas City office was brought in to work on the design of the stadium seating bowl, drawing on his experience of a number of American projects. The stadium design team would soon expand to include the engineering practice Mott MacDonald, who were appointed as engineers responsible for both structure and services.

Despite the initial enthusiasm, Angus Campbell of Foster + Partners recalls the months after winning the appointment as rather frustrating. The initial development of the design was dictated by English Heritage's requirement to preserve the northern frontage and the iconic towers. However, it was obvious to the design team that retaining the towers for anything other than sentimental reasons was utterly illogical and would add considerably to the cost of the project, not least because a new stadium of 80-90,000 seat capacity would occupy a much larger footprint than the existing structure and would dwarf whatever remained of the original building. But pressure to preserve the towers came from several quarters. Leading figures from English football joined the lobby seeking to save these 'landmarks of the country'; and *New Civil Engineer* magazine went so far as to publish a series of proposals from respected engineers, arguing for their retention.

01

02

03

01 The World Stadium Team's first design for the new Wembley Stadium, presented publicly in 1999, was for a masted structure that retained the old stadium's east-west axis. It was obvious to the design team that retaining the twin towers for any reason other than sentiment was illogical and would invite considerable cost increases.

02 A new national stadium as first imagined by Foster + Partners for Wembley Stadium in 1995. This scheme retained the twin towers as a gateway to an extended stadium plaza leading to an arena with a cable net structure.

03 This early scheme for Wembley had a principal approach from the north, with new facilities accommodated on land to be acquired behind the old stadium. This would have required a significantly larger site than was ultimately available.

The first thing that we as a team with the client asked ourselves was what constitutes the best of its kind in the world today? How can we create a new generation stadium? How can we learn from previous stadiums? What form does it take? The project had to be conceptually robust and flexible enough to withstand many challenges, financial and political. NORMAN FOSTER, PRESENTATION AT THE ARCHITECTURE FOUNDATION, LONDON, 22 MAY 2007

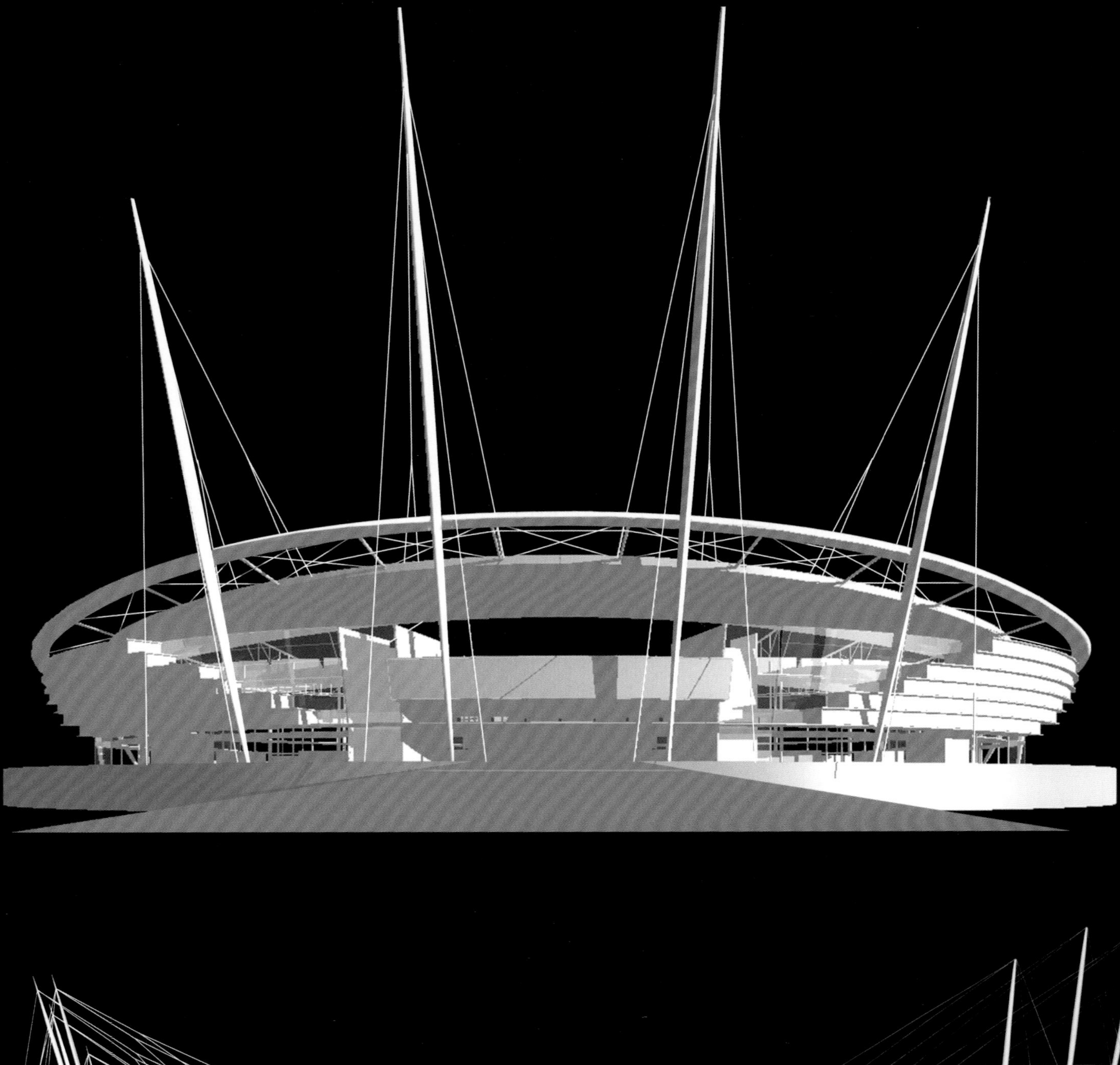

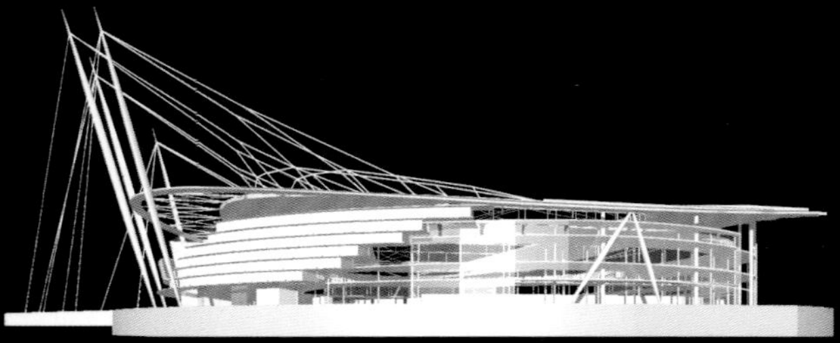

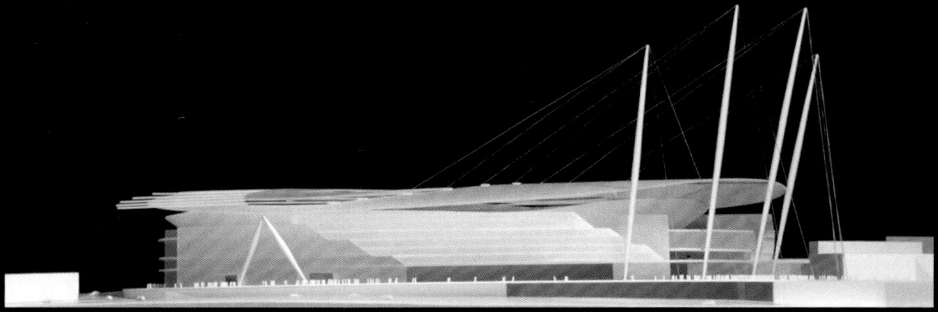

Above — The first World Stadium Team proposals for Wembley featured four 130-metre-high masts supporting a retractable roof capable of covering all 90,000 seats. However, the main concern was to design a stadium that had a sense of theatre, recapturing some of the old Wembley's atmosphere and sense of occasion. The design team began to have doubts about the masted scheme: was it distinctive enough; was it special to Wembley?

By 1999, as a result of prolonged negotiations coordinated by planning consultant Nathaniel Lichfield & Partners (and a report which estimated the cost of moving the towers to accommodate the new stadium at a prohibitively expensive £20 million), English Heritage had come to accept the idea of total demolition. 'Substantial community benefits' – the creation of around 8,000 jobs and the generation of £300 million of investment in the area – were legitimate arguments for accepting the loss of a listed building. The compensation should be 'a replacement stadium of an outstanding quality of contemporary design, well integrated into its setting, and evoking the landmark qualities of the existing building'. Aware of the new stadium's potential to act as a catalyst for the wider regeneration of the area Brent Council, the local planning authority, was also hugely supportive of the project.

However, the battle was not yet won. The number of seats the new stadium should provide remained a key issue. Ken Bates and Bob Stubbs were adamant that the stadium could only work financially if a substantial area of seating was provided for corporate hospitality – as many as 16,000 seats. But that met with resistance from the Sports Council and the government – 'they would talk about the common man and the democratic aspect of it', Stubbs recalls. 'But our argument was that the Lottery had only put in £120 million. If the government wanted to give us another £200 million then we would have happily rejigged the design.' Ken Bates' ideal was a 100,000 seat stadium – the more seats there were, he argued, the better chance the ordinary fan had of getting into a game.

In fact, Bates wanted to expand the brief for the building even further, with a 2,000-seat restaurant, hotel and offices incorporated into the stadium: if Chelsea Village had worked, why could there not be a Wembley Village? The hotel and offices were later deleted from the project, but the hospitality element remained and was expanded to become the fundamental ingredient in terms of the stadium's business plan. As Bob Stubbs comments, 'the whole stadium was designed around our corporate hospitality requirements: without these, the stadium would never have paid its way'. The design brief was a 300 page document, which took a year to prepare but provided a detailed schedule of the required facilities, right down to the number of hooks in the changing rooms.

The old stadium had many shortcomings but there were some aspects of it that the architects sought to incorporate into its replacement – its atmosphere and sense of occasion, the famed trophy presentation route up to the Royal Box (the '39 steps'), and not least the famous 'Wembley roar'. What became clear very early on was that Wembley was going to be a new kind of stadium. 'We started with a blank piece of paper', says Alistair Lenczner, one of the most passionate football fans in the design team. 'Our major concern was that the stadium should have a sense of theatre.'

One fundamental element of the brief was that all seats should be covered. Another was the FA's insistence that the pitch should be natural grass, though artificial surfaces had been laid in some recent stadiums and were becoming more acceptable to both UEFA and FIFA. Maintaining a healthy grass pitch requires adequate light and ventilation. 'The design challenge was to maximise the amount of natural light and air at pitch level, within a large seating bowl, and with a roof covering every seat', says Lenczner. (At the San Siro stadium in Milan, where a third tier of seating had to be added for the 1990 World Cup, the installation of a new roof had caused the pitch to deteriorate markedly.)

Another consideration was to try to minimise the shadowing of the pitch for afternoon games. That essentially is how the idea of a partially retractable roof emerged; a roof that in its 'open' or 'retracted' position between events would allow maximum light and air to reach the turf, but in its 'closed' position could move forward to cover the seats. Furthermore, should the weather be clement enough for the roof to be left in its retracted position for a daytime event, the design would minimise shadow on the pitch.

During 1999 the design team developed designs for a 90,000 seat stadium (75,000 public seats, the rest for corporate hospitality) covered by a roof with retractable sections. The basic form of the bowl had been decided early on, with much input from HOK in the development of a tiered diagram that represented a break with the old Wembley stands. The roof during the initial stages was to be supported by four 130-metre-high masts positioned on the north side of the stadium. A number of recent stadiums – for example, the City of Manchester Stadium, Cardiff's Millennium Stadium, and the Stade de France – have roofs supported by masted structures. The form had been pioneered by Frei Otto and Günter Behnisch in the striking stadium designed for the 1972 Munich Olympics.

When the designs for the new stadium were launched at Wembley on 29 July 1999, Chris Smith was guest of honour and praised the scheme. However, Banks' replacement as sports minister by South London MP Kate Hoey was soon to usher in a rapid cooling of relations between WNSL and the government with the provision for athletics the main issue in dispute.

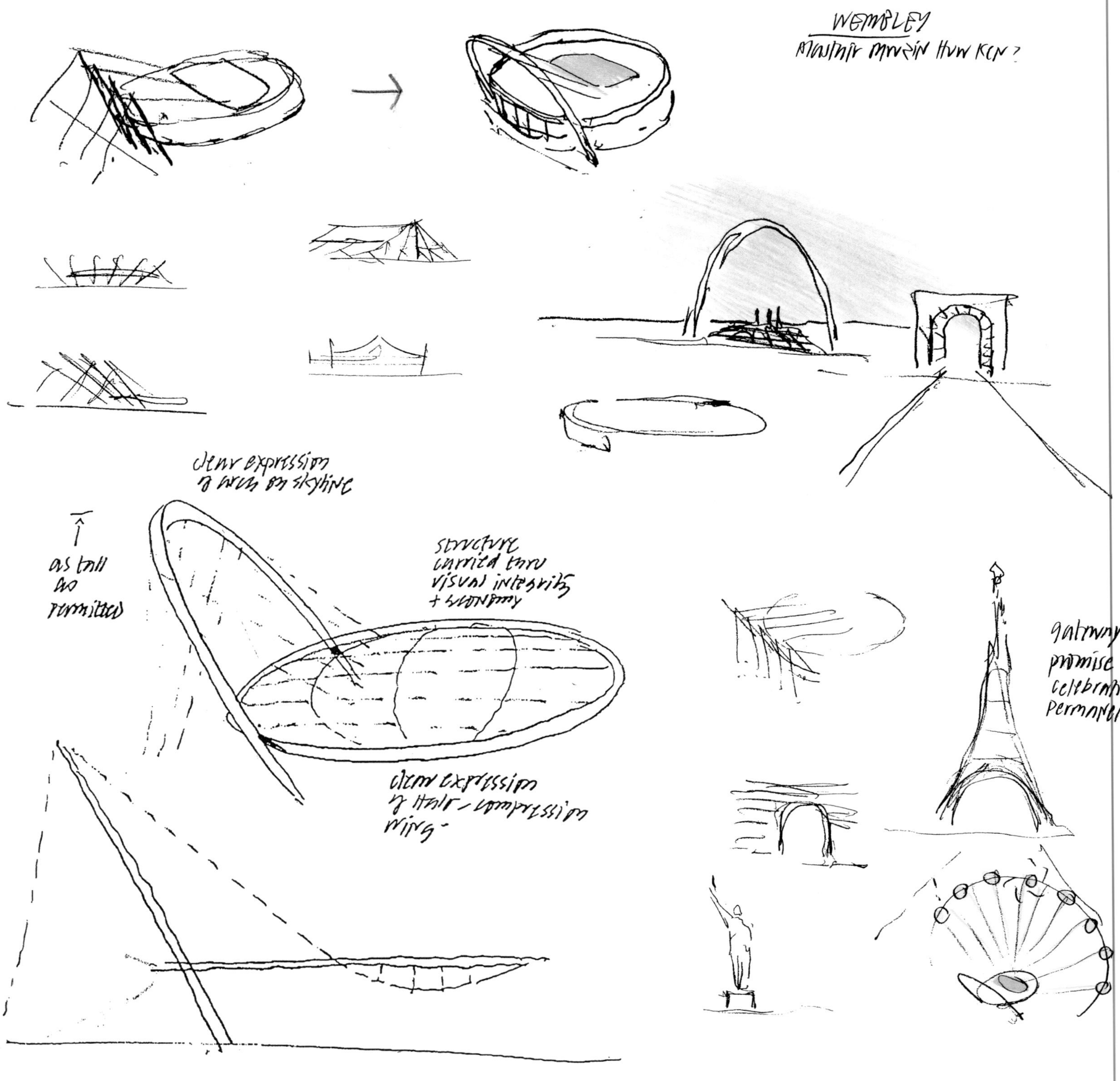

When we launched the scheme it was still a masted structure. But I don't think I was alone in having some concerns about the image it presented – it wasn't special to Wembley. The day after our press conference – a Saturday – I was cycling in the countryside in Germany. It was then that I decided we had to do better. That was how the arch began. Over the course of that weekend there was a frantic exchange of sketches, by fax, between myself and Alistair Lenczner, an engineer in the office in London. Remarkably, in those early sketches, he anticipated the eventual height of the arch to within a metre. NORMAN FOSTER, PRESENTATION AT THE ARCHITECTURE FOUNDATION, LONDON, 22 MAY 2007

Paris's Stade de France, constructed with generous state funding to house the 1998 World Cup, had provision for a running track to be installed by making the lower tier of the seating bowl retractable in sections. Bob Stubbs visited the Paris stadium and discovered that the inclusion of retractable seating had added up to £40 million to the cost of the building. Ken Bates was adamantly opposed to a similar arrangement at Wembley: a large area beneath the stands would need to be set aside for back-of-house storage facilities, sacrificing space, he argued, that was needed for bars, toilets and other facilities. Why build in something that might never be used, or at best be used once in 50 years?

It was Rod Sheard, a senior partner in HOK Sport and a key member of the design team, who came up with an alternative suggestion – the installation of a temporary concrete platform above the football pitch. Such a platform would extend over as much as 20 rows of seating but still provide enough capacity for the largest international athletics meeting as well as a temporary football pitch. An athletics arena constructed on a permanent elevated concrete platform had already been built at the Stade Louis II in Monaco and Bates took Derek Casey, the chief executive of the Sports Council, to see it in action. It seemed to work well. So Bates resolved to adopt the same strategy at Wembley: 'since it was my stadium and not the government's, who weren't putting any money into the construction, then I was going to do it my way', he insisted. Should it ever be required, a temporary installation would involve some cost (approximately £12 million according to Sport England's report on the stadium's athletics design) and take several weeks, but it would give Wembley the potential to house major track and field events when called upon to do so – at a tiny fraction of the cost of a new stadium.

However, the athletics platform solution did not satisfy Kate Hoey, the athletics lobby or the British Olympic Association. Chris Smith was persuaded to commission an independent report into the stadium's athletics capability, which was prepared by American architects (and stadium specialists) Ellerbe Becket. Their report was critical of the new stadium design on a number of counts, leading some to conclude that it would be unsuitable as an athletics venue. Norman Foster says the report was 'shot full of holes', while Rod Sheard points out that it compared Wembley – not primarily planned for Olympics use – with purpose-built Olympic stadiums. The matter was debated in the House of Commons. There was even talk of the FA being forced to repay the £120 million Lottery grant. Eventually, on 22 December 1999, even though WNSL had never been given the opportunity to counter the allegations made in the report, Chris Smith announced that Wembley would not be used for athletics, and that the site for an athletics stadium would be sought elsewhere in London. Nonetheless, Wembley Stadium still retains the ability to host major athletic events, through the installation of a temporary deck, should it ever be required.

Throughout this period, as the political battles rumbled on in the background, the design team had continued to develop the stadium. The decisive move was the abandonment of the masted scheme in favour of the great arch. It was a crucial change, creating a new landmark that more than compensates for the loss of the towers; but what prompted it?

England manager Kevin Keegan had been reported as complaining that the masted scheme looked too much like the Stade de France. Norman Foster had other doubts. He had questioned the scheme privately for some time. 'My worry was that the masted structure was not in any way special to Wembley and in fact had a lot of associations with other building types – the circus tent, for example', he says. The weekend immediately after the launch at Wembley Foster was in Germany, at the Bayreuth Festival. The decisive moment came while cycling in the countryside above Bayreuth: he knew that a radical rethink of the project was required.

The idea of a 'super arch' emerged in a rapid exchange of faxes with Alistair Lenczner during the course of that weekend. For Foster, the arch was a symbolic structure that expressed 'promise, celebration, permanence'. He developed sketch ideas while Lenczner worked out how such a structure could be constructed on a very tight site – the height of the arch was a determining factor. First thing on Monday morning Mouzhan Majidi briefed the Foster model shop to make a rudimentary foam model of the arch proposal. As soon as the model was ready he took it to show to Rod Sheard and his colleagues. 'To his great credit, Rod wasn't upset that we were having second thoughts about the scheme, just a few days after unveiling it. In fact he immediately supported the new design', Majidi recalls. But the client's support was also vital.

Now back in London, Norman Foster took a set of sketches on the arch idea to show to Ken Bates at Stamford Bridge. Bates thought the arch was terrific – a great improvement. He saw immediately that with the masts and many of the cables removed, there would be fewer constraints on the design of the concourse spaces. It would also be far more economical in terms of the amount of structural steel required compared to the previous masted designs. With the form of the arch agreed, the team moved on to develop ways of constructing it.

Opposite — Some of Norman Foster's early Wembley sketches. Through these sketches, Foster begins to outline a landmark building, a triumphant arch and a strong symbol for the new Wembley – an iconic image as distinctive to London as the Eiffel Tower is to Paris.

A number of stadiums designed by HOK and LOBB over the previous decade or so had featured arch-shaped trusses – the Telstra Stadium (formerly Stadium Australia) in Sydney, for example, or, on a more modest scale, the Galpharm Stadium in Huddersfield. (Oscar Niemeyer's unrealised 1941 stadium project, which featured a parabolic arch of concrete, was not known to the design team at this stage.) But in these projects arches had been developed with a structural role as deep curved trusses, in effect, supporting the forward edge of the roof of a single stand. Wembley's single arch works as a more pure compression structure, appearing as a freestanding element clearly silhouetted against the sky. It supports all of the seating bowl's north roof and 60 per cent of the weight of the south roof. For structural precedents one has to look to the field of bridge design: the bridges of Gustave Eiffel, for example; or nearer to home, the Tyne Bridge in Newcastle.

Sketches by Norman Foster done during the course of August envisaged the arch as 'a tiara ... triumphant, inviting, a gateway – an emblematic symbol'. Impressive by day, at night the arch would be 'an illuminated jewel', lit using a sophisticated lighting scheme. Several weeks of intensive work during that same month saw the arch idea developed by the architects in consultation with the engineering team from Mott MacDonald, led by Steve Morley. Working with Alistair Lenczner, the Mott team evolved more detailed designs for the roof structure, including a methodology for incorporating a sliding roof.

The planning process moved steadily forward during late 1999 and early 2000. A planning application was submitted to Brent in February 2000 and planning permission was granted in May. On 7 October that year, the last match was played in the old stadium, with Germany beating England 1–0 in a World Cup qualifier under a brooding grey sky – a disappointing final chapter to its three quarters of a century as the crucible of English football. Thereafter the stadium was closed to await demolition and redevelopment, although as it turned out, work would not start on site for another two years.

Funding was the key issue at this point. Ken Bates stood down as chairman of WNSL at the end of 2000. His departure from WNSL followed unsuccessful attempts to secure the necessary finance from a series of banks, who were not convinced by the business plan, demanding still further corporate hospitality provision, and worried by the government's attitude. (Cordial relations between the two parties would not be resumed until the departure of Chris Smith and Kate Hoey in the reshuffle following the 2001 election, to be replaced by Tessa Jowell as Secretary of State and Richard Caborn as sports minister.)

Bates was a controversial figure but won the respect of the stadium's design team, enjoying – in his own words – 'a bloody good relationship' with Norman Foster. Certainly his achievement in transforming a vision into the reality of the new Wembley was profound. He had already brought in the big Australian contractor Multiplex (which had worked on Chelsea's stadium) to tender for the project, at a price, it was later to emerge, that seriously underestimated the real cost. But, though the project was to create huge problems for Multiplex, its founder and chairman, John Roberts (1934-2006), was to play a key role in its realisation. For Norman Foster, Roberts and Ken Bates were the prime movers – 'without those two individuals, the project would not have happened', he says.

According to Ben Vickery of HOK Sport, 'John Roberts made the stadium project work. He put Multiplex in the driving seat'. The contractual basis of the project was to be a design and build arrangement, with the architects and other consultants 'novated' to Multiplex, who became in effect their client. Two major banks had failed to assemble financial packages for Wembley. Where they failed, Robin Saunders of the German commercial bank West LB succeeded.

Saunders, persuaded by Roberts to take on Wembley, began negotiations with WNSL and other bodies to cement the contractual agreements that would make Wembley pay. One idea was to sell the name of the stadium, which is common practice in the world of sport, but this possibility was precluded under the terms of the Lottery funding agreement. Saunders' approach was coolly financial: 'I didn't want to get lost within the passion for the game or the passion for the national stadium', she says. In September 2002, WNSL signed up to a £426 million loan extending over 16 years from West LB and was able to finalise its own contract with Multiplex.

Thus, the project was effectively 'relaunched' in 2002 after having been in limbo for a year or more. Work started on site on 30 September that year, and demolition work took six months. The last things to go were the towers, torn down ceremoniously by the largest demolition machine available, nicknamed 'Goliath'. 'It was a cheering sight', says Alistair Lenczner. 'It meant there was no turning back.'

One of the constraints on the project was the tightness of the site. The adjacent land had been sold to a developer, which was not prepared to allow access to its property. The tubular steel arch,

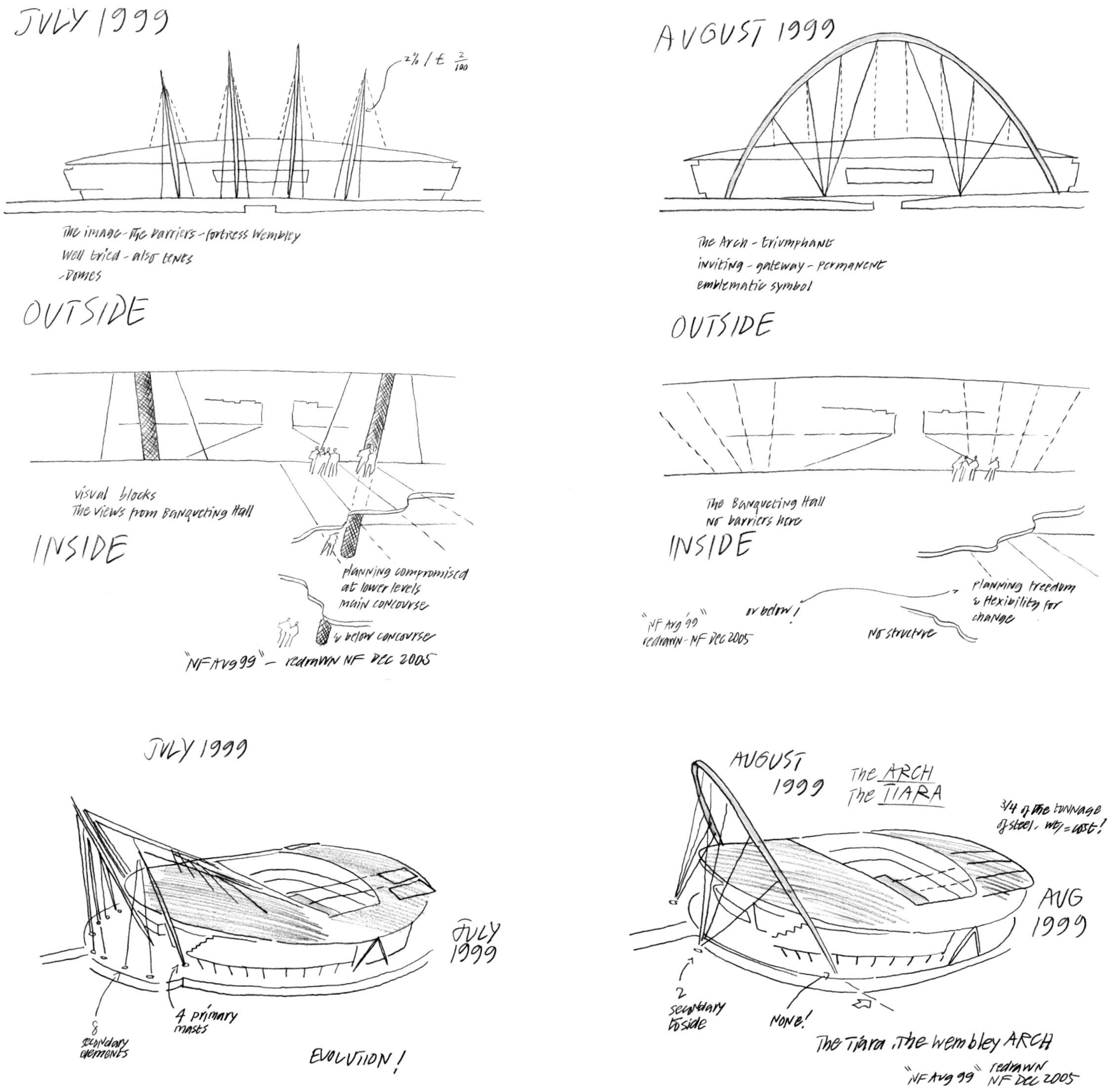

bove — Some of Norman Foster's more developed Wembley sketches in which he charts the evolution from a masted structure to an arch, and notes the many advantages of the new structure. In one frenetic month, from July to August 1999, the design team developed this idea, testing and refining it along the way.

Norman has a culture in his office that doesn't get hung up on holding on to an idea. Nobody tries to defend ideas that to be honest have outlived their usefulness. You change it and change it and change it until the very last minute when you can't change it any longer. Then you know that it is as good as you can possibly do. That's what happened with Wembley. ROD SHEARD, PRESENTATION AT THE ARCHITECTURE FOUNDATION, LONDON, 22 MAY 2007

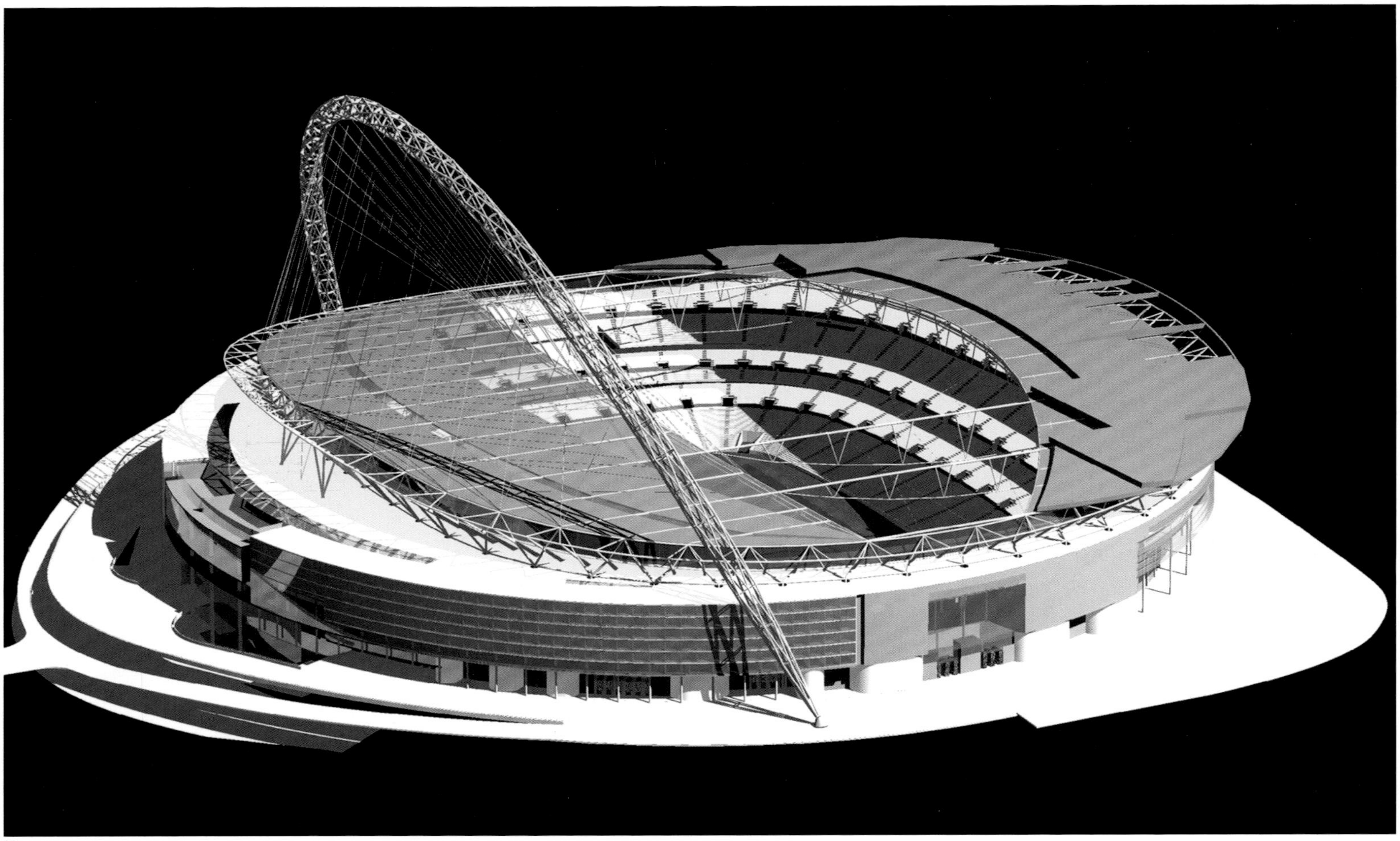

01

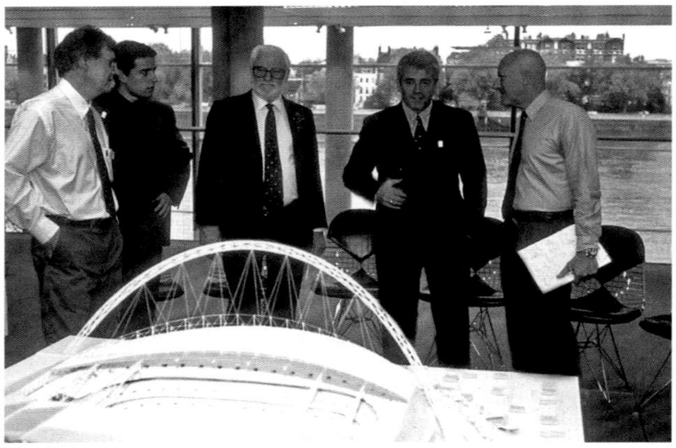

02

03

Looking at the original masts, I thought, 'Hang on, how big are these things – I can't have these bloody great things, blocking the view of my restaurant'. A few days later, Norman comes over to the Chelsea Stadium bar, orders a bottle of champagne, and pulls out some sketches of the new scheme. He says, 'What do you think?' I was gobsmacked. It was so much better. But then I thought, what's the cost implication? He said 'It's neutral.' So I said: 'Do it'. KEN BATES, IN CONVERSATION WITH THE EDITOR, 2005

01 This early visualisation of the new stadium illustrates the four acres of sliding roof panels on the south side and the arch to the north, with the pitch oriented east-west to maximise the distribution of sunlight. The panels would eventually be resolved as two separate units.

02 The arch scheme is presented to the FA and FIFA as part of England's bid for the 2006 World Cup. From left: Ken Shuttleworth, Nick Barron of the FA, Ken Bates, England football team manager Kevin Keegan and Norman Foster.

03 Norman Foster, Ken Bates and FIFA representatives discuss the arched stadium.

spanning 315 metres and rising 133 metres high, therefore had to be constructed on the future site of the pitch. The arch was prefabricated on the ground by Cleveland Bridge, the company which (as Dorman Long) had constructed both the Sydney Harbour Bridge and the Tyne Bridge. (Cleveland Bridge was subsequently replaced by Hollandia as a result of a dispute with Multiplex that was to develop into a protracted legal wrangle.)

The arch, weighing 1,750 tonnes, was raised into position in the summer of 2004. It became an instant landmark and shortly afterwards road signs to the new stadium went up, featuring the arch logo. For a year and a half, however, it supported nothing but its own weight and was held in place by five huge temporary restraining cables. With the installation of the main roof structure below the arch the time came (in December 2005) to 'de-prop' the arch so that it could fulfil its structural role. With the roof now supported by the arch, cladding could be applied during the course of 2006 and the retractable roof panels on the south, east and west sides of the stadium installed, increasing the total weight of the roof to around 7,000 tonnes. The drive mechanism for the retractable roof panels as finally installed by Hollandia was developed as a powered rack and pinion system, rather than a cable system which was considered less robust.

Like the arch, everything about the new stadium is big in scale: 688 food and drink service points, for instance, and more than 2,600 lavatories (a six-fold increase on the provision in the old stadium). Extending 305 metres east-west and 300 metres north-south, the new stadium has a significantly larger footprint than its predecessor. The seating bowl is made up of three main tiers. The lower tier, accessed from the lower concourse, seats about 35,000. The middle tier, including club seats, hospitality suites and the Royal Box (now approached by 107 steps) accommodates some 16,000 people. The top tier, reached by lifts, stairs and escalators (the latter common in American stadiums but rare in Europe) seats approximately 39,000.

One of the key features of the new stadium is the fact that everyone, not just those paying top prices for their seats, can enjoy facilities as good as those in any sports venue in the world. In some respects, in fact, the top tier seats offer the most dramatic views of any in the stadium and there is an external terrace at level 5 overlooking Olympic Way and open to all in the top tier. Most of the spectator facilities are contained in a six-storey 'drum', a very large building in its own right, which wraps around the whole stadium.

A service road at basement level provides 360-degree vehicle access for all the stadium's operational or service vehicles, including television trucks, and also provides a secure point of entry for players, officials and VIPs. (The segregation of public and private spaces was a key issue in the design programme.) From the outset, the new stadium was conceived as a public transport destination, shifting the emphasis away from travel by car, and prompting considerable investment in upgrading the local transport infrastructure. The stadium can be accessed from either Wembley Stadium or Wembley Central overground and Underground stations, but most people arrive at Wembley Park Underground station and walk along the processional route of Olympic Way. It is from here that you really appreciate the full impact of the great arch.

The principal hospitality spaces and restaurants, with seating for 10,500 people, look out over Olympic Way – the deletion of the hotel and offices from the earlier schemes allowed more space for dining rooms and function rooms. Two restaurants, as well, of course, as the 163 private boxes, each with its own bar, servery and WC, look directly out on to the pitch. The stadium's main internal lower concourse is a huge public space, circled by an outer ring of kiosks and cafés. Spectators progress through the building via soaring naturally-lit spaces with views out, a far remove from the gloomy and enclosed interiors of older stadiums.

The pitch – Wembley's 'hallowed ground' – is naturally the heart of the new stadium. It lies 4 metres below the level of the old Wembley turf. The quality of the grass was a major issue and advice was sought from the Sports Turf Research Institute. Experts oversaw the laying of the new pitch in June 2005, using turf specially grown in Lincolnshire. The quality of the grass is ensured by underground drainage and ventilation systems, the latter ducting fresh air through the roots to encourage growth. Hot water pipes provide protection against frost in winter.

When rock concerts or other such events are staged – the first a performance by George Michael with a capacity audience – the pitch is covered with specially designed protective panels, creating a space in which more than 20,000 people can stand. The stadium's sophisticated sound system can be used for concerts, which do not have to rely solely on sound projected from stage-based equipment.

Provision for television coverage was another important design issue, given the fact that the bulk of the FA's income comes from television broadcasting. There are two permanent TV studios at the stadium and 70 hard-wired camera positions, including the main camera gantry and positions distributed on all sides of the seating bowl.

All of this was put to the test on 19 May 2007, when the new stadium hosted the eagerly awaited FA Cup Final between Chelsea and Manchester United. Although generally acknowledged as an unremarkable game – at least in the first half – the magic and excitement of Wembley itself was palpable. Hours before kick-off, Norman Foster was interviewed by a television crew on the roof of a nearby hotel. The view of the great arch was a novel one, even for him. But the fact that all the news crews wanted to use it as a backdrop revealed the degree to which it has already become established as the new symbol of a national institution – a national icon. Walking down Olympic Way with his wife and colleagues, Foster was stopped by a number of fans, who wanted his autograph, to snap a photograph of him with a child proudly sporting team colours, or simply to shake his hand. This was a good-humoured crowd, set to enjoy a great day out – everybody wanted to tell him how wonderful they thought the new stadium was.

The stadium absorbed the huge crowd quickly and efficiently. Full to capacity for the first time, it finally became the great forum that its designers had anticipated, surprisingly intimate despite its vast scale. The 'Wembley roar' was still there, so too was the essential thrill of the place. The stadium had passed its greatest test. Norman Foster summed this up very well when he said, 'the real skill in designing a stadium isn't the technical stuff. It's designing a building that bottles emotion'.

The new Wembley is a structure that embodies the drama and romance of sport. It represents nothing less than a transformation of the idea of the stadium. In some respects, of course, it is part of a global renaissance, represented, for example, by the Allianz Arena in Munich, constructed for the 2006 World Cup, and the Olympic Stadium in Beijing, the main venue for the 2008 Olympic Games. Sport is big business. Hosting the World Cup or Olympics, with their vast international audience, is a booster for the standing of cities and whole nations. In 2005, Britain's longstanding ambition to host the Olympics for the first time in more than half a century was realised with the announcement that the 2012 Games would be held in London. Over the previous decade, the possibility of Wembley acting as an Olympic venue had emerged again and again as the stadium project evolved. Ultimately, however, the decision was taken to construct a new stadium at Stratford in East London.

The new Wembley is already a popular London landmark – and like a World Cup victory it is the product of first-class teamwork. Its architecture and engineering excellence reflects that joint endeavour and the results will be enjoyed by millions of spectators in decades to come. For millions more who never enter the stadium, its great arch – visible for miles across London and beyond – is a powerful signal of the stadium's rebirth and a reminder of the dynamism and energy of a world city. The dream of creating an iconic visitor destination at Wembley, which the pioneer Edward Watkin first had back in the 1890s with his great Wembley tower, and which lived on in the twin towers of the old stadium, has been given new life. The new stadium has claimed its place on the global map as an international symbol of sporting and architectural excellence. A new chapter in Wembley's rich history has begun.

01

02

03

01 An early visualisation of the stadium on a match day, with the roof fully retracted.

02 Event day dressing – banners, posters and pennants – envisaged to overlay the neutrality of the stadium. Similarly, in the seating bowl, the fans' parade of team colours stirs Wembley to life.

03 High quality dining spaces are characterised by an undulating diagrid motif that recalls the diagonal bracing of the arch. Wembley's twelve restaurants range in size from 500 to 2,000 seats and are serviced by ninety-eight kitchens – the largest is one-third the size of the pitch.

Colour, by the way, has been deliberately spurned; the idea here is for the events and crowds themselves to add all the light, life and colour needed to bring this stately, steely-grey building to hugely animated life. By night, the stadium will light up – sporting a coat of many colours – while the great arch, visible from many miles, will shine above all. JONATHAN GLANCEY, THE GUARDIAN, 9 MARCH 2007

The demolition of the famous Wembley twin towers began at just after 2pm yesterday, the final act in a long drawn-out saga, and the most significant. Few could fail to spot the irony of a German excavator known as 'Goliath' being charged with the task.

Alan Pattullo, *The Scotsman* — 8 February 2003

MULTIPLEX
McGEE
McGEE
McGEE
JCB
MULTIPLEX

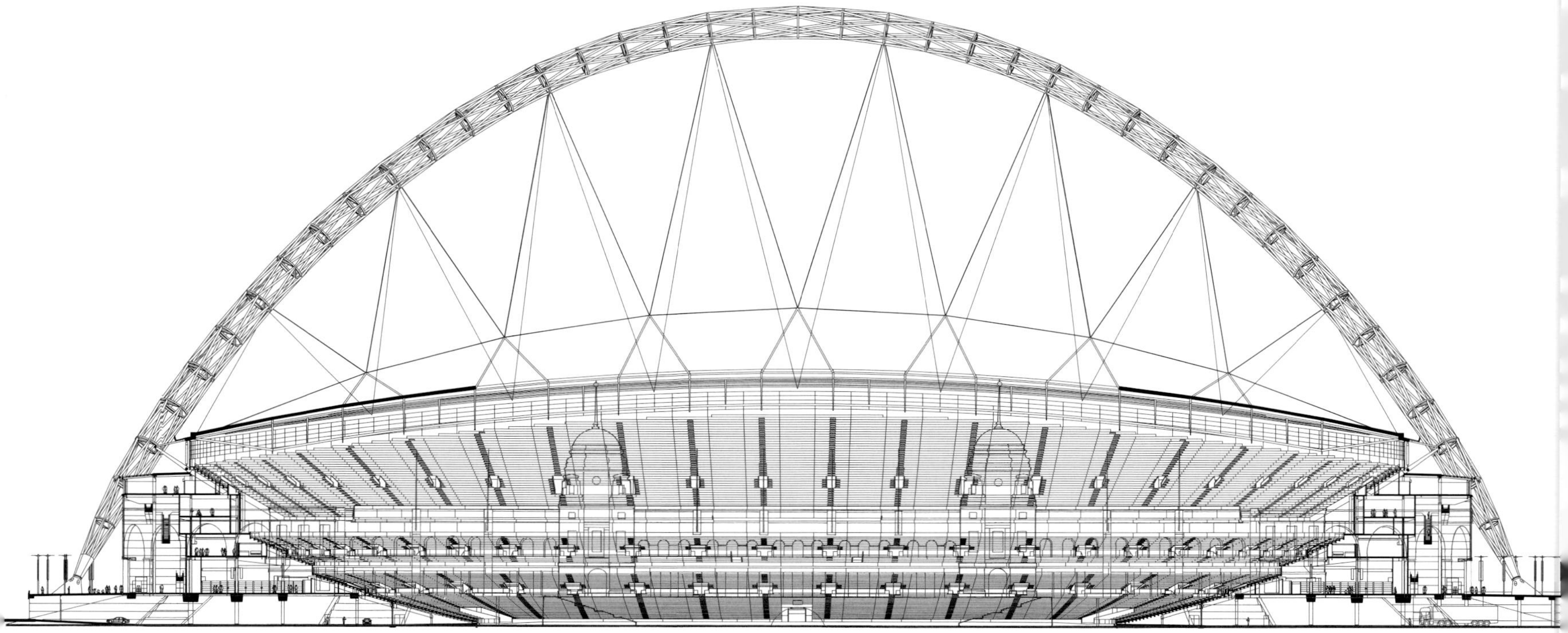

Previous page — The giant German excavator 'Goliath' starts to chip away the old stadium's remaining tower, 2003.

Above — An elevation of new Wembley Stadium compared with the old. Standing 133 metres high and spanning 315 metres, the arch is almost four times taller than the original twin towers. The longest single-span structure in the world, the 7.4-metre diameter structure is tall enough to roll the London Eye underneath and is wide enough to carry a Channel Tunnel train. At 1,750 tonnes, the arch weighs the equivalent of 275 double-decker buses or ten jumbo jets.

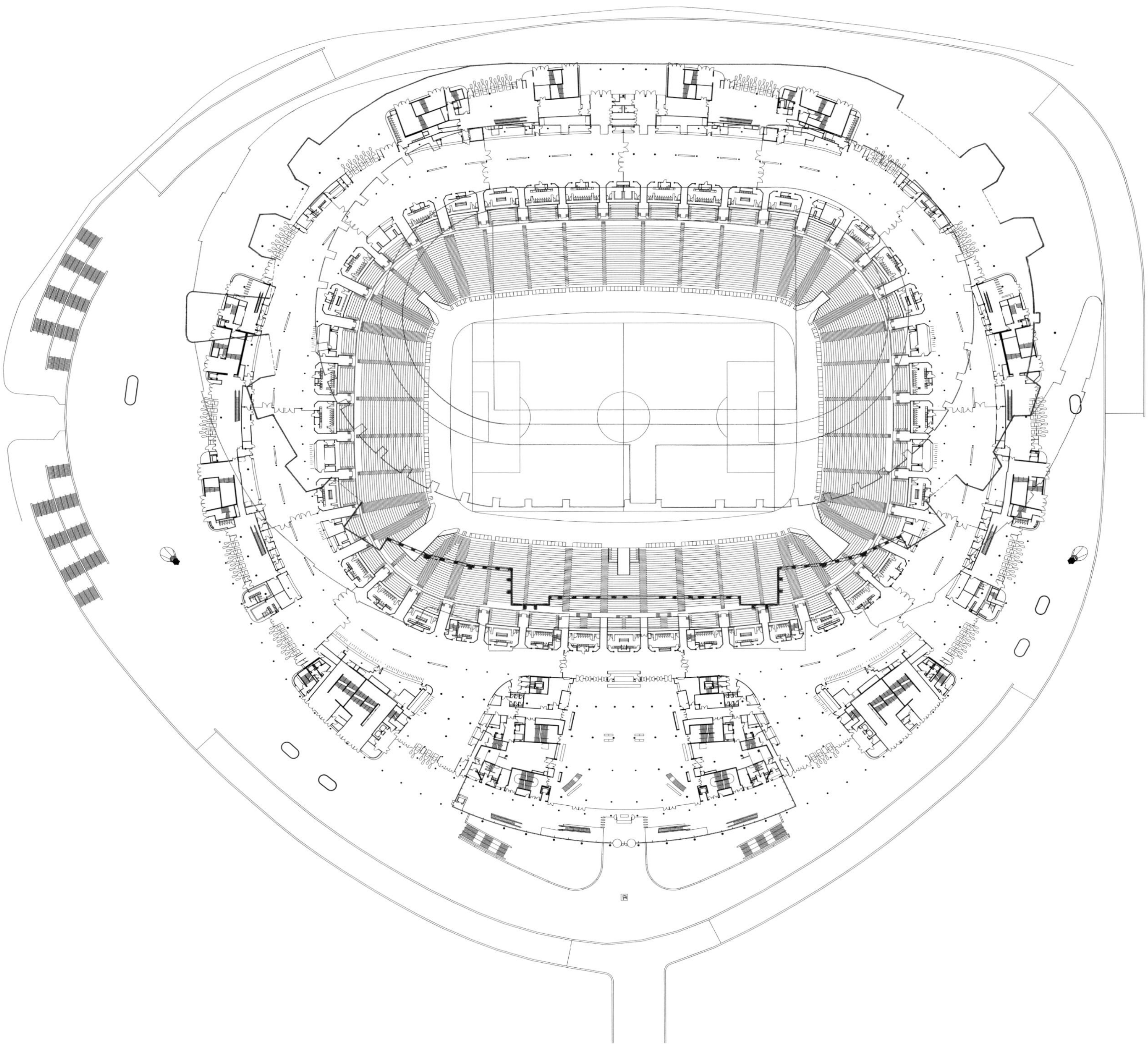

Above — A plan of the new Wembley Stadium compared with the old. Twice the size of its predecessor, the new stadium is among the most spacious and best equipped in the world. Every one of the 90,000 seats inside the new bowl has clear sight lines, a marked contrast with the 20 to 25 per cent of seats whose views were obscured by pillars in the old stadium.

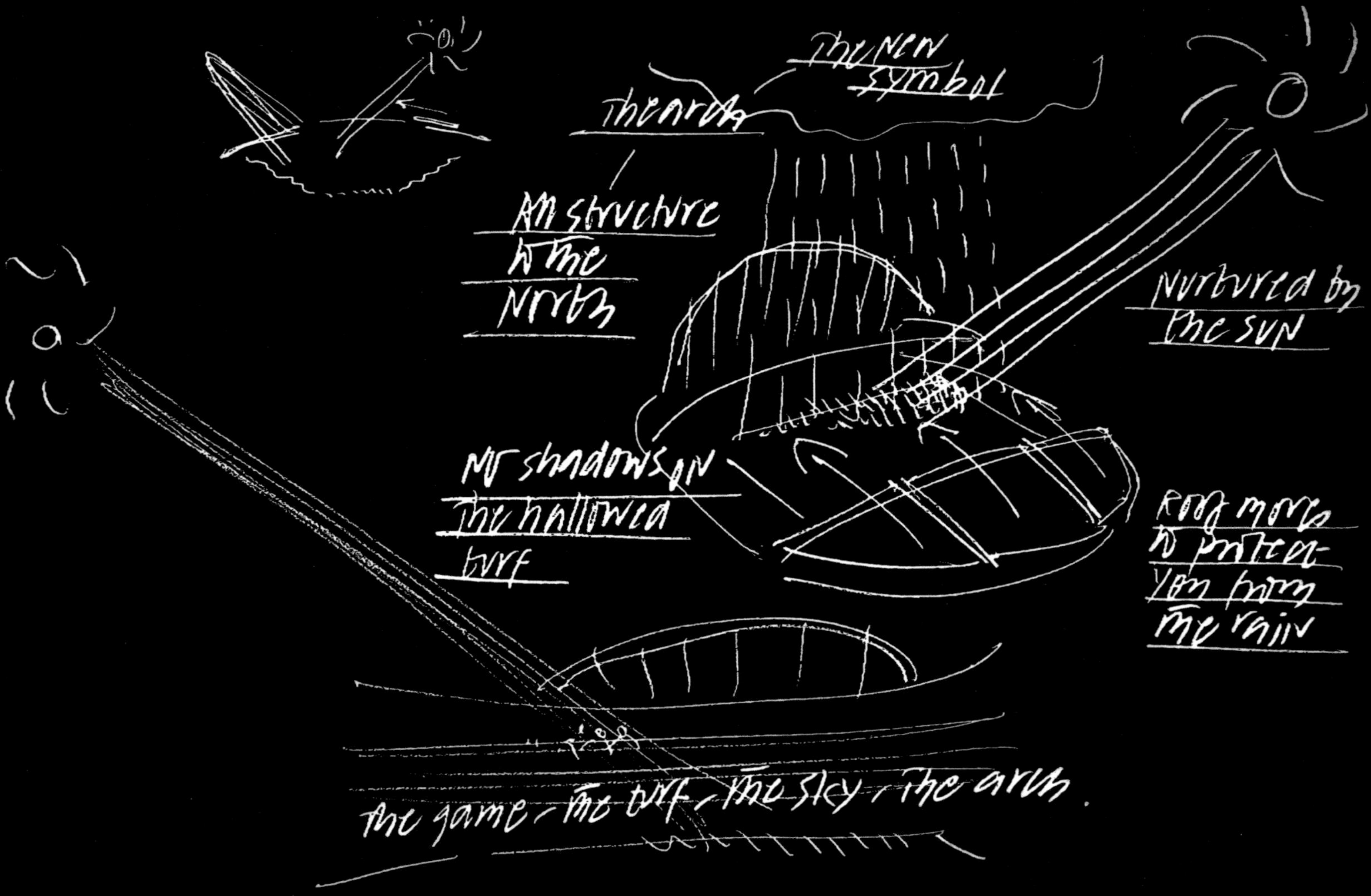

One of the key generators of the design of the roof was the 'hallowed turf'. The turf requires constant nurturing. Without sunlight and fresh air the grass will not grow. The question was how do you protect all 90,000 spectators from the rain, but in fine weather still allow air and sunlight to reach the pitch? The answer was a retractable roof, which operates as a series of sliding panels. NORMAN FOSTER, PRESENTATION AT THE ARCHITECTURE FOUNDATION, LONDON, 22 MAY 2007

Above — Sketches by Norman Foster explaining how the retractable roof would allow sunlight to fall on the pitch, an essential factor in maintaining healthy grass.

Opposite — Extracts from a sequence of sunlight studies, modelled at regular intervals throughout the day, with the roof open and closed. The design challenge was to maximise the amount of light and air at pitch level, while protecting spectators from the rain. Essentially, this led to the idea of a retractable roof; one that would cover the seating when required but also allow light and air to reach the turf and minimise shadow patterns on the pitch.

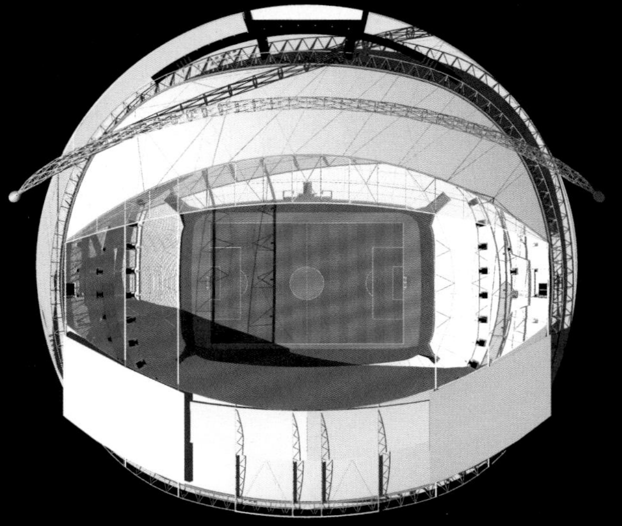

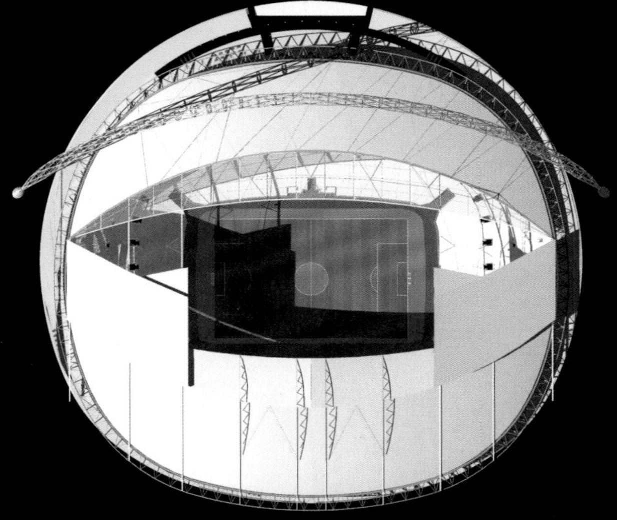

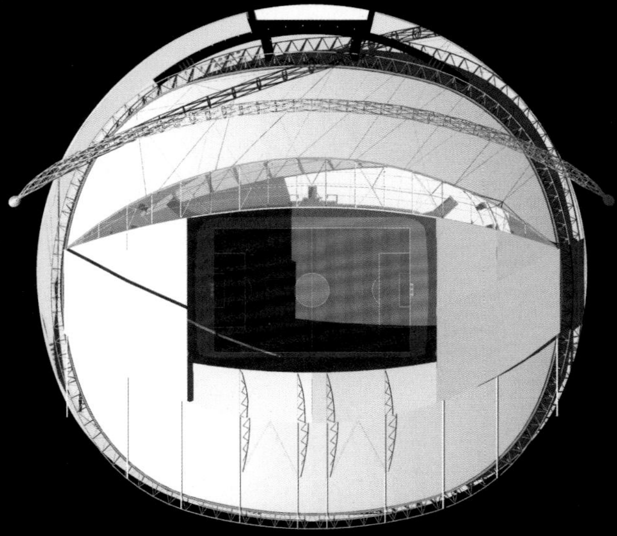

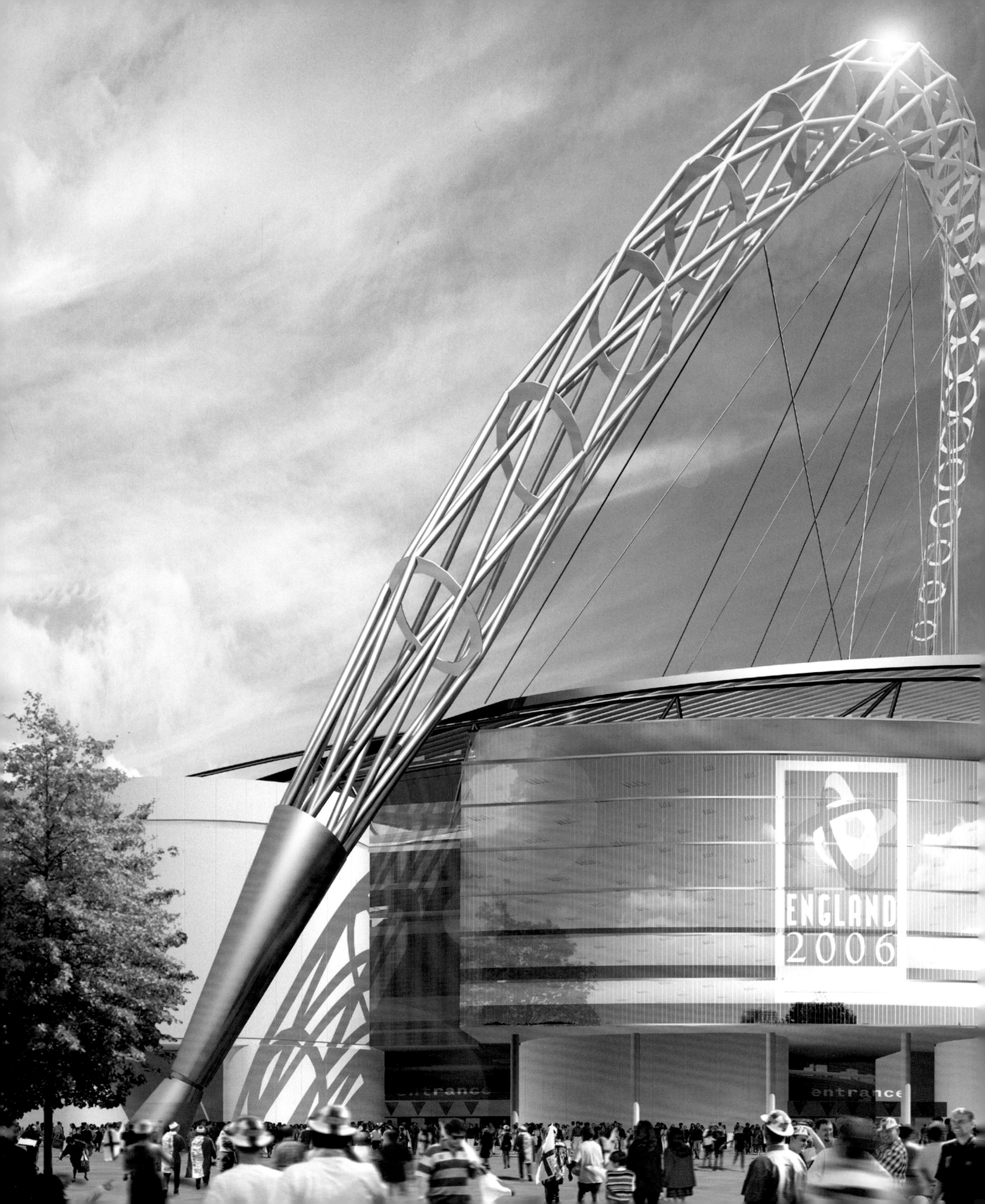
ENGLAND
2006
entrance
entrance

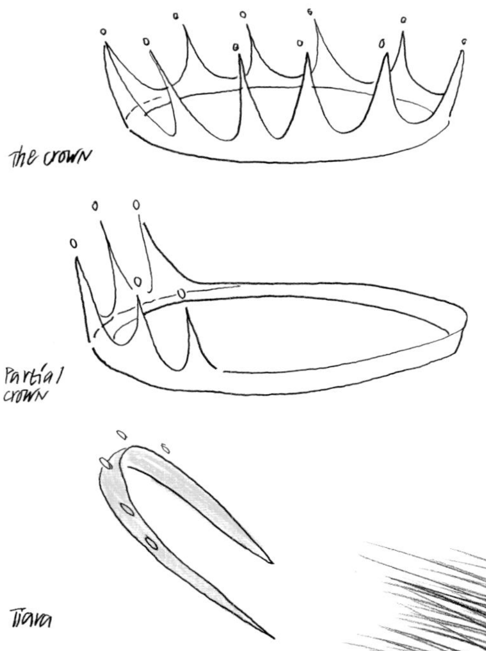

Reflective during the day, a symbol day & night.
UNIQUE, NO CONFUSION WITH OTHER STADIA
"NF Aug 99"
redrawn NF Dec 2005

Opposite — An early visualisation of the arch. Consisting of forty-one steel rings connected by spiralling tubular chords, the arch tapers at each end and is supported by concrete bases, founded on piles 35 metres deep. Inclined sixty-eight degrees to the vertical, the arch is held in position by a series of cables tied to the main stadium structure.

Above — In these sketches, Norman Foster explores the arch's symbolism: 'glistening at night on the skyline, a jewel, a tiara'.

Sport is a huge phenomenon around the world. A big match like the FA Cup Final will have an international television audience of something like 450 million people. So it's not surprising that with numbers like these a lot of money flows into football – enough money to finance a building like Wembley. But if you're going to create a major new stadium it has got to have an image that people will recognise instantly when they tune in. That's what these buildings are about. ROD SHEARD, PRESENTATION AT THE ARCHITECTURE FOUNDATION, LONDON, 22 MAY 2007

Above — An early masterplanning model of the stadium and its surroundings, including provision for an athletics warm-up track to the east of the arena (seen lower left in this image), which could be built should Wembley ever become a venue for a future Olympiad. This land has since been sold, but a potential warm-up track location exists in the shape of a public park, just across the Chiltern Railway line, to the south of the stadium.

Opposite — Elevational studies of the final stadium design. Restaurants, bars, entertainment and conference facilities form a 'drum' of accommodation, wrapped around the seating bowl. Rising above it, the 133-metre high, 315-metre long arch, described as a 'tiara' of steel, supports the retractable roof.

Overleaf — A cutaway drawing showing how the 'drum' of entertainment facilities and hospitality suites is arranged around the perimeter of the seating bowl. Escalators take spectators to the upper levels.

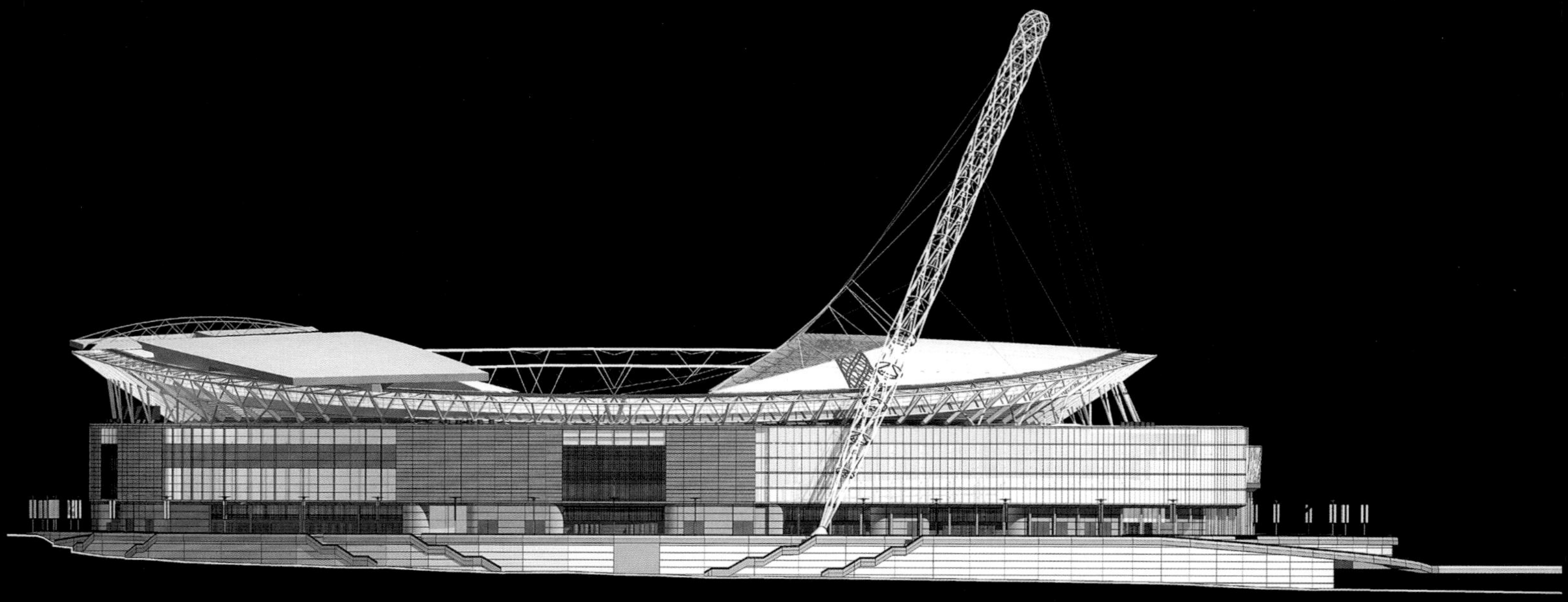

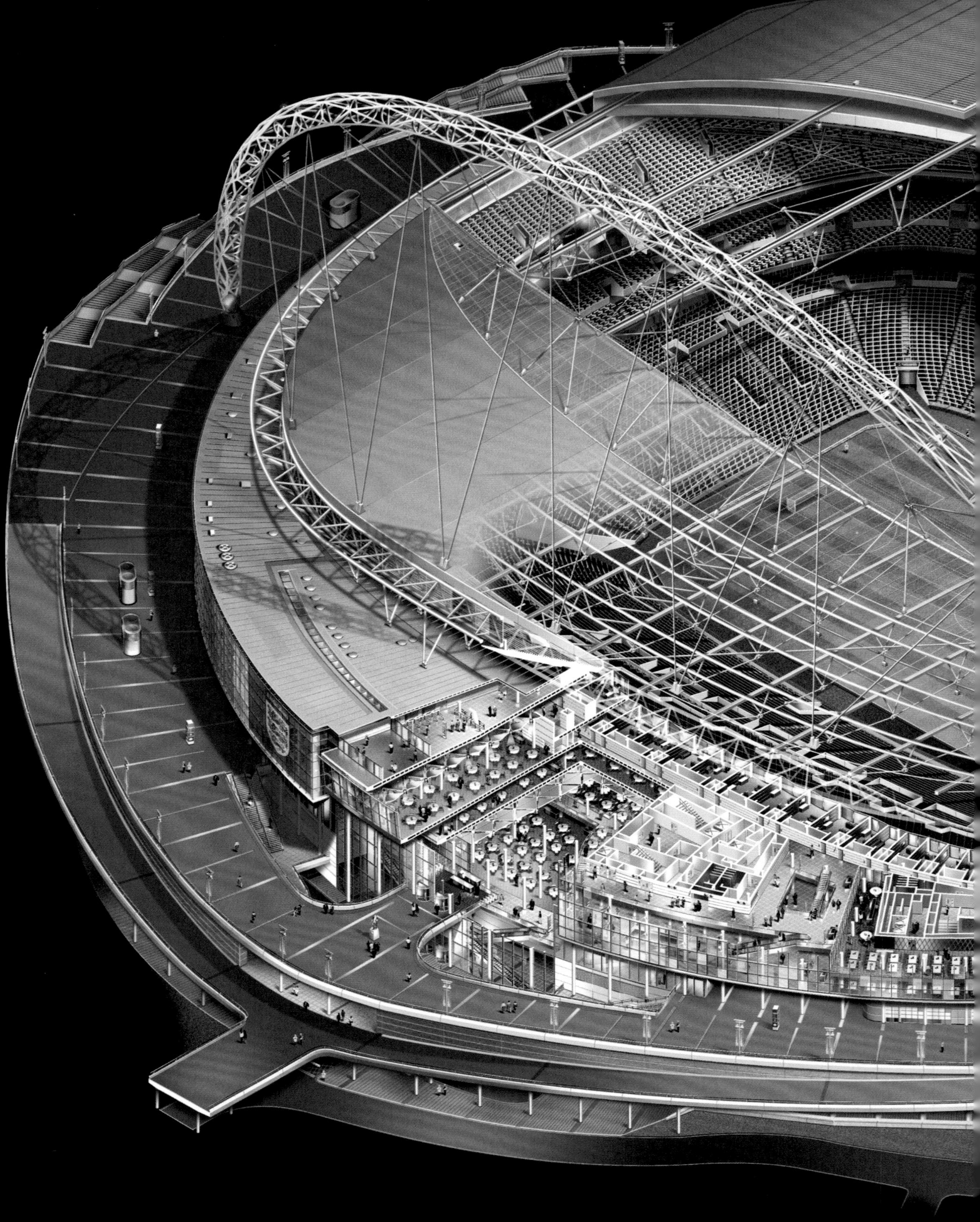

Drawing by Gregory Gibbon

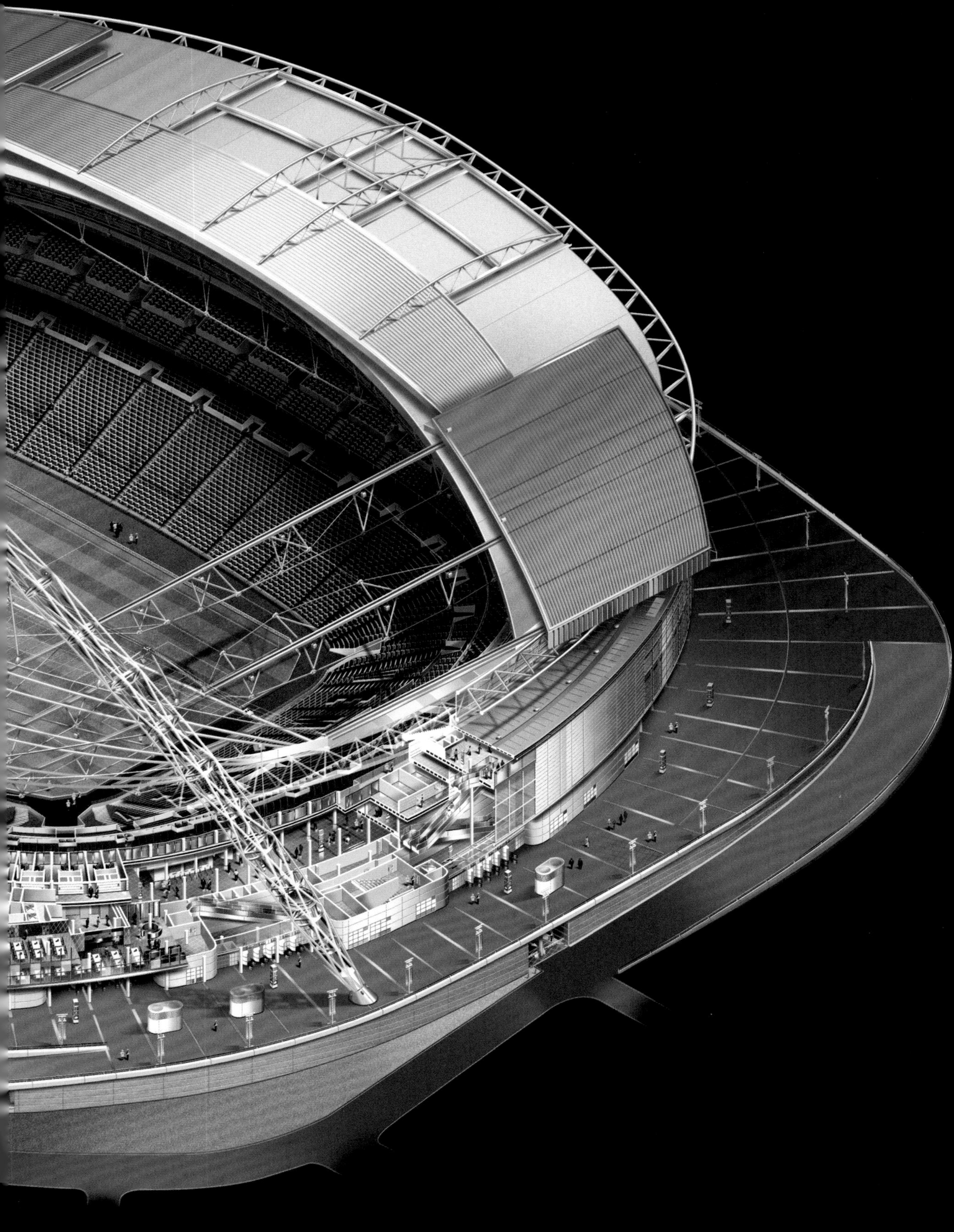

01

02

05

06

09

10

Multiplex got a terrible press over Wembley, but they built nothing but the best – every single time. Usually when a design-build contract starts, the builder comes to you and says: 'Right, how can we save money?' Multiplex never did that. They never put pressure on us. Their attitude was 'If it's good – the best we can do – then that's what we are going to do.' ROD SHEARD, PRESENTATION AT THE ARCHITECTURE FOUNDATION, LONDON, 22 MAY 2007

01–11 A sequence of photographs taken from a fixed vantage point over a five-year period from the commencement of demolition of the old stadium in 2002 to the official opening in 2007.

03

04

07

08

11

From left to right, top to bottom. The final dawn for old Wembley; demolition begins on the west stand; remnants of the south stand and the towers are the last to go; stair cores for the new stadium begin to rise; fabricated inside four large red sheds, steel diagrid sections of the arch are assembled on the pitch; erection of the arch on the south side begins; temporarily vertical, the arch reaches its apex; five temporary stays anchor the arch while hefty concrete cores (visible in the foreground) prevent its release; the roof structure below the arch is substantially complete; the arch supports the completed roof structure; finally, the building is ready for its first game.

01

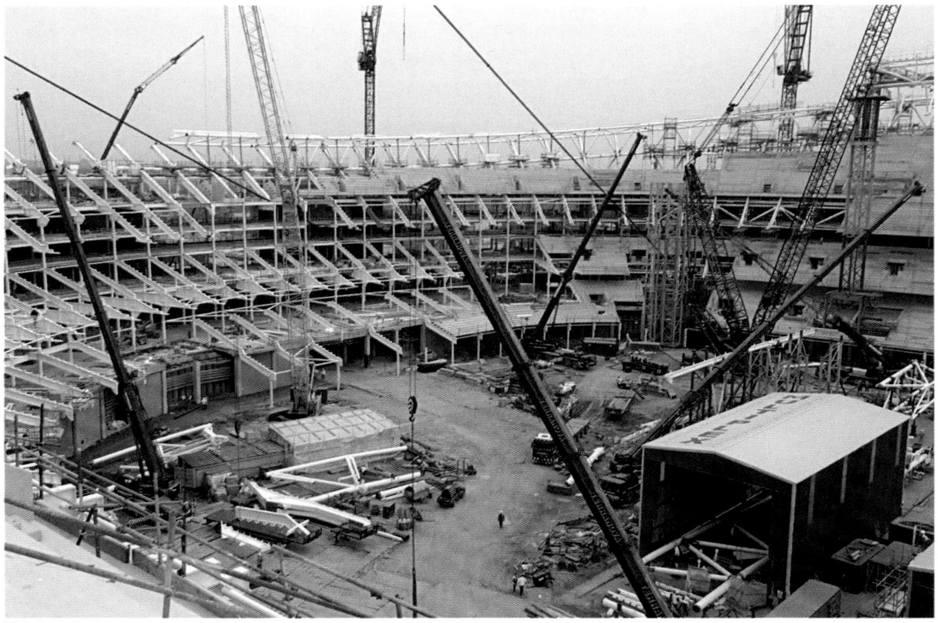
02

03

04

01 At its peak, the construction of the stadium involved over 3,000 employees on site, overseen by members of the World Stadium Team. Here, architect Norman Foster (left) and engineer Alistair Lenczner inspect the newly raised arch.

02 With limited space available outside the stadium, the pitch became a fabrication space for elements of the arch and the perimeter truss. Simultaneously, the bowl grew up around it.

03 Pre-cast concrete terracing is secured to the steel bowl structure.

04 The tubular steel rakers that support the upper tier on the south side. In all, the new stadium is comprised of thousands of such components, amounting to some 23,000 tonnes of structural steel.

Opposite — In order to secure the arch from the north after its trajectory from the south, massive temporary arch stays penetrated the stadium bowl edges. Upon their removal, several segments of terracing in the bowl required back-filling with pre-cast concrete tiers.

01

02

03

It is easy to romanticize the old stadium with its cramp-inducing wooden seating and evil-smelling toilets, which went out of fashion when Thomas Crapper was a boy. Yet Sir Norman Foster's tiara, an arch big enough for a Channel Tunnel train to pass through, has quickly replaced the twin towers as an international icon. MICHAEL CALVIN, SUNDAY MIRROR, 20 MAY 2007

01 The completed stadium, seen from the south-west. The Wembley Arena is in the foreground.

02 Arch assembly begins on the south side.

03 Elements of the arch arrived from Darlington and were welded together in the four central sheds to form ring units; each of the units was lifted into place to form the 315-metre long 'tiara' of steel.

04

05

06

04 The stadium seen from the west. The roof is seen here fully open.

05 The arch is raised from the south, with gaps in the seating bowl allowing it to swing through smoothly.

06 The roof structure below the arch is assembled and the seating bowl is completed.

Overleaf — The stadium at night. Wrapped by a kilometre of internal concourse, each of the three tiers of seating anticipates capacity crowds – the lower layer holds 34,303, the middle one 16,532 and the upper one 39,165. Placed end to end, the seats stretch to a distance of fifty-four kilometres and each is twenty-five per cent wider than the benches in the old stadium.

CHELSEA v MANCHESTER UNITED — 2007
FA Cup Final

Seven years after the bulldozers moved in on the stadium that Pelé once described as 'the church of football', 89,826 customers finally had the chance to pay homage to the national game at the gleaming, arched cathedral that replaced it.

Simon Hart, *The Sunday Telegraph* — 20 May 2007

Arena
Restaurant
& Bar
Open

01

02

03

Previous page — The FA Cup Final comes home as Chelsea and Manchester United meet at Wembley on 19 May 2007. Framed by the distinctive Wembley arch, fans and rivals again bring Olympic Way alive with colour.

01, 02 Fans queue at the turnstiles.

03 The 6-metre-high statue of Sir Bobby Moore by sculptor Philip Jackson pays tribute to one of England's greatest footballers. Moore made 108 appearances for England, 642 appearances for West Ham and was Footballer of the Year in 1964, Sports Personality of the Year in 1966 and was awarded the OBE in 1967.

The plaque at his feet reads: 'Immaculate footballer. Imperial defender. Immortal hero of 1966. First Englishman to raise the World Cup aloft. Favourite son of London's East End. Finest legend of West Ham United. National Treasure. Master of Wembley. Lord of the game. Captain extraordinary. Gentleman of all time.'

04

05

06

07

04–07 The light-filled atrium on the north side provides vertical circulation to the hospitality areas and also acts as a pre-function gathering space. Escalators, which are uncommon in British stadiums, transport fans right to the upper reaches of the tiers.

The easy circulation accords with Ken Bates' view: 'At St James' Park in Newcastle and at Old Trafford you suffer a bloody heart-attack climbing all the stairs! I wanted ordinary punters to be able to get to the upper tier without killing themselves.'

01

02

03

On Saturday I went up to Wembley on the tube with the Manchester fans. As you pass Neasden you catch a glimpse of the arch. I could tell when it came into view because everybody who was standing leaned down to look out of the window. These Mancunians had been jibing each other the whole trip. But suddenly they went silent. Then I heard: 'Oooohhh, it makes you proud to be English doesn't it?'

ROD SHEARD, PRESENTATION AT THE ARCHITECTURE FOUNDATION, LONDON, 22 MAY 2007

01, 04 One of several publicly accessible cafés that together can cater for 10,500 seated meals at every event.

02, 03 Broad and spacious, the lower concourse circulation for general admission easily accommodates a thronging football crowd.

04

05

06

05 London's largest banqueting space, the Great Hall, seats up to 2,000 guests and overlooks the great processional route of Olympic Way. It is joined by five other premium venues, each of which offers an unprecedented level of service and dining at Wembley.

06 Hospitality areas flank the north side and open to the 163 corporate boxes. Each holds up to twenty guests and all have spectacular views of the pitch.

Overleaf — A fitting opening for Wembley. The Red Arrows soar overhead before kick-off for the 2007 FA Cup Final.

The energy behind The FA Cup

e·on
The energy behind The FA Cup
TheFA.com
PRESTON NORTH END
NOTTS COUNTY

01

02

03

04

05

It is what goes on on the turf that gives a stadium its patina. Old Wembley made its legends. The White Horse Final; Stanley Matthews in those baggy shorts dancing Blackpool back from the grave; England's World Cup and 'It is now'; lucky winners, gallant losers; the football chants of the Twin Towers and the hallowed turf. This afternoon they are playing not just for a cup and a medal. It is sentimental and monumental. THE TIMES, 19 MAY 2007

01 The Manchester United and Chelsea teams line up for the National Anthem before an expectant crowd.

02 Play begins beneath Wembley's spectacular fully retractable roof.

03 Manchester United fans reignite the famous 'Wembley roar'.

04 Chelsea goalkeeper, Petr Cech, performs in football's capacious new home.

05 United star Ronaldo displays his famous step-over.

06

07

08

06 Didier Drogba of Chelsea wheels away after his 116th-minute goal beats Edwin van der Sar of United. It was the only goal of an otherwise disappointing 2007 FA Cup Final.

07 Chelsea fans celebrate Drogba's winning goal.

08 After a climb up the 107 processional steps to the Royal Box, captain John Terry ecstatically lifts the Cup for Chelsea. The team is unique for winning both the last FA Cup Final at the old Wembley and the first in the new stadium.

Wembley's arch is conceived as a triumphal gateway – a heroic symbol for the new stadium. Floodlit at night, it is a new London landmark. You can see it soaring on the skyline from the very heart of the city.

Norman Foster, interviewed on BBC TV — 19 May 2007

BT

01

02

03

04

05

06

Previous page — the Wembley Stadium arch, radiant on the London skyline.

01 Wembley's new state-of-the-art facilities await the Three Lions before their first international match against Brazil, 1 June 2007.

02 The English and Brazilian teams file out of the tunnel.

03 An animated full house welcomes the teams on to the pitch.

04 David Beckham displays his trademark free kick.

05 English captain, John Terry, arrives at the back post to finish with a powerful header beyond Helton.

06 Terry's great Wembley run continues as he becomes England's first international scorer at the new Wembley stadium.

07

08

09

The arena itself is breathtaking. A vast undulating wave of sculpted concrete, set about with 90,000 red plastic seats, each with plenty of leg room and uninterrupted views, it shelters beneath a gigantic yet unobtrusive roof, all 11 acres and 7,000 tonnes of it supported by Foster's 133-metre high, 315-metre long 'tiara' of steel. JONATHAN GLANCEY, THE GUARDIAN, 9 MARCH 2007

07 A St George's cross formation celebrates England's national pride during the first international match against Brazil at the new stadium, 2007.

08 England's finest, Steve Gerrard, slides in to tackle Brazilian star Kaká.

09 The last gasp. Denying England a debut win at Wembley, Brazil's late equaliser saves their unbeaten seventeen-year run against the Three Lions.

01

02

03

04

05

I found myself looking not at the lonely-looking figure of Michael but at the remarkable stage setting behind him, with its giant rolling screen that curled from ceiling to floor. Even more compelling though, was the sight of this extraordinary stadium with its own elegant curves; it looked sensational and sounded terrific, too. The stage was a stunning piece of visual engineering which, as evening moved into night time, became a thing unto itself, a feast of colour and pattern ... But for me, above all, the night belonged to Wembley: warm, resonant, friendly, the stadium was the star. DAVID CHEAL, THE DAILY TELEGRAPH, 11 JUNE 2007

01–05 George Michael plays Wembley's first concert, 9 June 2007. The new Wembley event stage is London's ultimate big-name music venue – a dramatically different venue from the one he performed in with Wham! for Live Aid.

06

07

08

06 Originally the first scheduled performance at the New Wembley Stadium, British band Muse plays to an effusive audience for their first major stadium debut, 2007.

07 As it was for Muse's concert, a temporary platform can be erected above the pitch for events, bringing fans as close as possible to the stage. With a higher roofline and purpose-built sound system, the new stadium. is a premier entertainment venue.

08 The Concert for Diana celebrated the People's Princess on what would have been her 46th birthday. Many of her favourite pop and rock artists appeared, followed by a performance of *Swan Lake*, Act Four, which recalled Diana's love of ballet, 2007.

Overleaf — Illuminated to celebrate the first FA Cup Final, Wembley Stadium's arch is seen reflected in the waters of Brent Reservoir. The arch is lit by 258 metal halide floodlights mounted within the structure. The internal face of the lattice structure becomes an arc of light that grows more diffuse towards the edge and reads as a halo hovering above the stadium.

Chronology

1922 Construction of Wembley Stadium begins. Designed by Sir John Simpson and Maxwell Ayrton, engineered by Owen Williams, it is built by Sir Robert McAlpine in just 300 days. It forms the centrepiece of the British Empire Exhibition and the stands have a capacity of 120,000.

1923 First FA Cup Final between Bolton Wanderers and West Ham United on 28 April 1923. Bolton win 2–0, but the match is marred by 200,000 people (rather than the anticipated 120,000) turning up to watch, the crowd spilling on to the pitch where they are dispersed by PC George Scorey and his white horse 'Billy'.

1924 The Empire Exhibition is opened by King George V, on St George's Day, 23 April. The exhibition cost £12 million and was the largest exhibition ever staged anywhere in the world, attracting 27 million visitors.

1924 The first international match is held in the stadium, England draws 1–1 with Scotland.

1925 The Empire Exhibition closes.

1926 Ex-serviceman Arthur Elvin buys the stadium.

1929 Wembley hosts the annual rugby league Challenge Cup Final and the Greyhound St Leger.

1936 Wembley hosts the first World Speedway motorcycle championships.

1937 Sunderland v Preston is the first FA Cup Final filmed by television cameras before the fixture is broadcast live the following year.

1939 The last Cup Final before the War is won by Portsmouth 4–1 against Wolves (Wembley hosted Cup Finals in each of the war years).

1941 Prime Minister Winston Churchill is introduced to the players on the pitch before England beats Scotland 2–0.

1942 Hundreds of servicemen and women descend on Wembley for a series of Christmas parties.

1944 Dwight D Eisenhower is the guest of honour as Charlton beat Chelsea in the League Final South.

1945 France are England's first foreign opposition at Wembley, drawing 2–2.

1947 State of the art greyhound photo-finish equipment is installed.

1948 Wembley hosts the major track events of the XIV Olympiad. London had originally been granted the 1944 event but could not act as host because of the Second World War. Czech distance runner Emil Zátopek and Dutchwoman Fanny Blankers-Koen are the stars.

1951 England beats Argentina 2–1 – the first South American team to play at the stadium in a match celebrating the Festival of Britain.

1951 Wembley hosts the first England women's hockey matches – and continues to host these games from 1951-1969, and again from 1971-1991.

1953 The 'Matthews' Final', supposedly the greatest FA Cup Final at Wembley. Stanley Matthews inspires his Blackpool team to come back from 3–1 down to win 4–3 against Bolton Wanderers.

1953 Hungary becomes the first foreign team to win at Wembley, the great Puskás inspiring his team – the 'Magical Magyars' – to a 6–3 victory.

1954 Billy Graham hosts a Christian 'crusade' in front of 120,000 people.

1955 Floodlighting is introduced to the stadium.

1957 Chairman Sir Arthur Elvin dies after running Wembley for thirty years.

1960 England are named as hosts of the 1966 World Cup, with the final to be staged at Wembley.

1963 AC Milan beat Benfica 2–1 in Wembley's first European Cup Final.

1963 Cooper v Clay World Heavyweight non-title fight. Clay beats Cooper in the fifth round.

1963 England plays a World team to mark the centenary of the Football Association. A new aluminium roof is installed above the whole stadium.

1965 West Ham beats Munich 2–0 in the stadium's first European Cup-Winner's Cup Final.

1966 England beats West Germany 4–2 after extra time in the final to win the World Cup. Geoff Hurst scores a hat trick. Captain Bobby Moore collects the Jules Rimet trophy.

1968 Manchester United – in a team featuring Bobby Charlton, George Best, and Dennis Law, and managed by Matt Busby – beats Benfica 4–1 in extra time to win the European Cup.

1972 Wembley's first pop concert features Bill Haley, Little Richard and Billy Fury.

1975 Bobby Moore's last Wembley appearance ends in defeat, with West Ham beating Fulham 2–0.

1981 To celebrate the 100th FA Cup Final, all the surviving captains take part in a parade 45 minutes before kick-off.

1982 Pope John Paul II celebrates mass before 93,000 at the stadium.

1983 American NFL teams play at Wembley for the first time, Minnesota defeating St Louis 28–10.

1985 Live Aid concert.

1986 Sir Brian Wolfson acquires the Wembley complex from BET and establishes Wembley plc, which he chairs until 1989.

1991 Tottenham Hotspur with Paul Gascoigne beat Arsenal 3–1 in the first FA Cup Semi-Final to be staged at Wembley.

1995 Frank Bruno out points Oliver McCall over twelve rounds at Wembley to become the WBC Heavyweight World Champion.

1998 Wembley plc sells Wembley Stadium to the FA for £120 million. The FA creates a subsidiary company Wembley National Stadium Ltd (WNSL) to run the stadium and commences plans for its rebuilding.

2000 England loses 1–0 to Germany in England's last match at the old stadium. Manager Kevin Keegan immediately resigns. Dietmar Hamann of Germany scores the last ever goal there.

2000 Planning permission is granted for the new Wembley Stadium. It is designed by the World Stadium Team (WST), a partnership between Foster + Partners and HOK Lobb.

2002 Demolition of the old stadium begins.

2003 Piling for the foundations of the new stadium commences. The piles go down as far as 35 metres – as deep as the original twin towers were tall. Earth works also reduce the level of the site – the new pitch is 6 metres below the level of the old playing surface. The twin towers are demolished on 7 February, the last elements of the old stadium to fall.

2004 Wembley's new arch is assembled. Weighing 1,650 tonnes it supports the 7,000 tonne retractable roof. The arch reaches its final position on 24 June, soaring 133 metres above the pitch.

2006 The projected opening of the stadium in time for the 2006 FA Cup Final is postponed.

2007 The stadium is complete and hosts a series of warm-up events during March and April. The Chelsea v Manchester United FA Cup Final is staged on 19 May 2007, Chelsea winning 1–0

Facts and Figures

0 Pillars or columns to obstruct spectators' views.

1 Kilometre, the circumference of new Wembley.

1 Time capsule that was buried under the pitch in December 2005.

1 Access cart that can be driven through the inside of the arch to allow routine inspections and maintenance to be carried out.

1 Special beacon, which is fitted on the apex of the arch to act as a warning to low-flying aircraft.

1 Bronze statue of Bobby Moore.

2 Giant screens, each the size of 600 domestic television sets.

2 Pairs of changing rooms, with a warming-up area in-between each pair.

3 Interior concourses, with each one having a one-kilometre circumference.

3 Tiers of seating, with the lower tier holding 34,303 spectators, the middle one 16,532 and the upper one 39,165.

4 Metres lower down – the pitch at new Wembley compared with that of the old stadium.

5 Years that the new stadium took to build.

7.4 Metres, the diameter of the arch, which is wide enough for a Channel Tunnel train to pass through.

8 Different floor levels, including the pitch as well as spectator and hospitality areas.

11 Acres, the size of the roof. Four acres of the roof are moveable.

20 First-aid rooms.

50 Centimetres, the standard seat width, compared to 41 centimetres in the old stadium.

52 Metres, the height to which the stadium roof rises above the pitch.

54 Kilometres, the length of the rows of seating if they were placed end to end.

68 Degrees, the angle that the arch stands from horizontal.

80 Centimetres, the standard depth of a seat, compared to 64 centimetres in the old stadium.

80 Kilometres of speaker cable.

87 Kilometres of security cable.

98 Kitchens, with the biggest one being one third the size of the pitch.

100 Trains an hour that can arrive in the vicinity of the new stadium on a major event day.

107 Steps that the players climb to collect their trophies from the Royal Box, as opposed to thirty-nine steps in the old stadium.

130 Kilometres of fire-alarm cable.

133 Metres, the height of the arch above the level of the external concourse. The twin towers at the old stadium were 35 metres high.

150 Toilets designed for disabled access.

310 Spaces for wheelchair users (and 310 companions), as opposed to 160 at old Wembley.

315 Metres, the span of the 'steel-tiara' arch, which is the longest single-span roof structure in the world.

380 Pitch floodlights.

400 Metres, the combined length of the escalators.

500 Security zones.

688 Food and drink service points; there were 152 in the old stadium.

1,294 Hand-wash basins.

1,750 Tonnes, the weight of the steel in the arch, which is as much as 275 double-decker buses or ten Jumbo Jets.

2,000 Jobs created in the construction period.

3,500 Catering staff on major event days.

4,000 Piles that form the foundations of the new stadium.

5,450 Pounds, the cost of an annual Corinthian Season Ticket, excluding VAT.

6,000 People employed on a major event day.

7,000 Tonnes, the weight of the roof.

7,000 Smoke/heat detectors.

7,500 Permanent jobs that are being created by economic activity directly related to the stadium.

10,500 Available seated meal covers per event, including capacity for 2,000 guests in the capital's largest banqueting hall.

12,000 Tonnes of pulling force required to raise the arch into place, which is the equivalent pulling strength of a fleet of 6,000 four-wheel drive vehicles.

17,000 The number of seats that are dedicated to Club England.

21,000 Sprinkler heads.

22,161 Tonnes of stone, gravel, sand and soil used to create the pitch.

23,000 Tonnes of structural steel used in the stadium construction.

50,000 Gallons of water that can drain through the pitch in one hour.

90,000 Seats, with every one of them pointing towards the centre circle.

165,000 Pounds, the average annual cost of a corporate hospitality box.

180,000 Square metres of internal floor space.

4,000,000 Cubic metres of space inside Wembley's walls and under its roof. It would take 25,000 double-decker buses or seven billion pints of beer to fill it.

40,000,000 Pounds, the amount that the Exchequer will receive each year from stadium-related activity.

229,000,000 Pounds, the total expenditure by visitors that is expected per annum.

XIV Olympiad — Medallists

BASKETBALL

Final

United States	65–21	France
Brazil		Bronze

BOXING

Flyweight

Pascual Pérez ARG	DEC – Gold
Spartaco Bandinelli ITA	Silver
Han Soo-Ann KOR	Bronze

Bantamweight

Tibor Csík HUN	DEC – Gold
Giovanni Battista Zuddas ITA	Silver
Juan Venegas PUR	Bronze

Featherweight

Ernesto Formenti ITA	DEC – Gold
Dennis Shephard SAF	Silver
Aleksy Antkiewicz POL	Bronze

Lightweight

Gerald Dreyer SAF	DEC – Gold
Joseph Vissers BEL	Silver
Svend Wad DEN	Bronze

Welterweight

Július Torma TCH	DEC – Gold
Horace Herring USA	Silver
Alessandro D'Ottavio ITA	Bronze

Middleweight

László Papp HUN	DEC – Gold
John Wright GBR	Silver
Ivano Fontana ITA	Bronze

Light Heavyweight

George Hunter SAF	DEC – Gold
Donald Scott GBR	Silver
Maurio Cia ARG	Bronze

Heavyweight

Rafael Iglesias ARG	KO 2 – Gold
Gunnar Nilsson SWE	Silver
John Arthur SAF	Bronze

CANOEING

Men's Canadian Pairs 1000m

Jan Brzák-Felix & Bohumil Kudrna TCH	5:07.1
Stephen Lysak & Stephan Macknowski USA	5:08.2
Georges Dransart & Georges Gandil FRA	5:15.2

Men's Canadian Pairs 10,000m

Stephen Lysak & Stephan Macknowski USA	55:55.4
Václav Havel & Jirí Pecka TCH	57:38.5
Georges Dransart & Georges Gandil FRA	58:00.8

Men's Canadian Singles 10,000m

Frantisek Capek TCH	1:02:05.2
Frank Havens USA	1:02:40.4
Norman Lane CAN	1:04:35.3

Men's Canadian Singles 1000m

Josef Holecek TCH	5:42.0
Douglas Bennett CAN	5:53.3
Robert Boutigny FRA	5:55.9

Men's Kayak Pairs 10,000m

Gunnar Åkerlund & Hans Wetterström SWE	46:09.4
Ivar Mathisen & Knut Östbye NOR	46:44.8
Thor Axelsson & Nils Björklöf FIN	46:46.2

Men's Kayak Pairs 1000m

Hans Berglund & Lennart Klingström SWE	4:07.3
Ejvind Hansen & Bernhard Jensen DEN	4:07.5
Thor Axelsson & Nils Björklöf FIN	4:08.7

Men's Kayak Singles 10,000m

Gert Fredriksson SWE	50:47.7
Kurt Wires FIN	51:18.2
Elvind Skabo NOR	51:35.4

Men's Kayak Singles 1000m

Gert Fredriksson SWE	4:33.2
Johan Kobberup DEN	4:39.9
Henri Eberhardt FRA	4:41.4

Women's Kayak Singles 500m

Karen Hoff DEN	2:31.9
Alida van der Anker-Doedens NED	2:32.8
Fritzi Schwingl AUT	2:32.9

CYCLING

1000-Metre Sprint

Mario Ghella ITA	2
Reg Harris GBR	0
Axel Schandorff DEN	Bronze

Time Trial

Jacques Dupont FRA	1:13.5
Pierre Nihant BEL	1:14.5
Thomas Godwin GBR	1:15.0

4000-Metre Team Pursuit

France	4:57.8
Italy	5:36.7
Great Britain	4:55.8

Road Race

José Beyaert FRA	5:18:12.6
Gerardus Voorting NED	5:18:16.2
Lode Wouters BEL	5:18:16.2

Team Road Race

Belgium	15:58:17.4
Great Britain	16:03:31.6
France	16:08:19.4

Tandem

Ferdinando Teruzzi & Renato Perona ITA	2
Reg Harris & Alan Bannister GBR	1
René Faye & Georges Dron FRA	Bronze

DIVING

Men's Platform

Sammy Lee USA	130.05
Bruce Harlan USA	122.30
Joaquín Capilla Pérez MEX	113.52

Men's Springboard

Bruce Harlan USA	163.64
Miller Anderson USA	157.29
Sammy Lee USA	145.52

Women's Platform

Vicki Draves USA	68.87
Patricia Elsener USA	66.28
Birte Christoffersen DEN	66.04

Women's Springboard

Vicki Draves USA	108.74
Zoe Ann Olsen USA	108.23
Patricia Elsener USA	101.30

EQUESTRIAN

Dressage

Hans Moser/Hummer SUI	492.5
André Jousseaume/Harpagon FRA	480.0
Gustaf-Adolf Boltenstern II/Trumf SWE	477.5

Dressage – Team

France	1269.0
United States	1256.0
Portugal	1182.0

Show Jumping

Humberto Mariles/Arete MEX	6.25
Rubén Uriza/Harvey MEX	8+0
Jean d'Orgeix/Sucre de Pomme FRA	8+4/38.9

Show Jumping – Team

Mexico	34.25
Spain	56.50
Great Britain	67.00

Three Day Event

Bernard Chevallier/Aiglonne FRA	+4.00
Frank Henry/Swing Low USA	21.00
Robert Selfelt/Claque SWE	25.00

Three Day Event – Team

United States	161.50
Sweden	165.00
Mexico	305.25

FENCING

Men's Épée

Luigi Cantone ITA	Gold
Oswald Zappelli SUI	Silver
Edoardo Mangiarotti ITA	Bronze

Men's Épée – Team

France	Gold
Italy	Silver
Sweden	Bronze

Men's Foil

Jehan Buhan FRA	Gold
Christian d'Oriola FRA	Silver
Lajos Maszlay HUN	Bronze

Men's Foil – Team

France	Gold
Italy	Silver
Belgium	Bronze

Men's Sabre

Aladár Gerevich HUN	Gold
Vincenzo Pinton ITA	Silver
Pál Kovács HUN	Bronze

Men's Sabre – Team

Hungary	Gold
Italy	Silver
United States	Bronze

Women's Foil

Ilona Elek HUN	Gold
Karen Lachmann DEN	Silver
Ellen Müller-Preis AUT	Bronze

FIELD HOCKEY

Final

India	4–0	Great Britain
Netherlands		Bronze

FOOTBALL

Final

Sweden	3–1	Yugoslavia
Denmark		Bronze

GYMNASTICS

Men's All-Around

Veikko Huhtanen FIN	229.70
Walter Lehmann SUI	229.00
Paavo Aaltonen FIN	228.80

Men's Floor Exercise

Ferenc Pataki HUN	19.35
János Mogyorósi-Klencs HUN	19.20
Zdenek Ruzicka TCH	19.05

Men's Horizontal Bar

Josef Stalder SUI	19.85
Walter Lehmann SUI	19.70
Veikko Huhtanen FIN	19.60

Men's Parallel Bars

Michael Reusch SUI	19.75
Veikko Huhtanen FIN	19.65
Christian Kipfer SUI	19.55
Josef Stalder SUI	19.55

Men's Pommel Horse

Paavo Aaltonen FIN Veikko Huhtanen FIN & Heikki Savolainen FIN	19.35

Men's Rings

Karl Frei SUI	19.80
Michael Reusch SUI	19.55
Zdenek Ruzicka TCH	19.25

Men's Team – Combined Exercises

Finland	1358.30
Switzerland	1356.70
Hungary	1330.85

Men's Vault

Paavo Aaltonen FIN	19.55
Olavi Rove FIN	19.50
János Mogyorósi-Klencs HUN / Ferenc Pataki HUN / Leo Sotorník TCH	19.25

Women's Team – Combined Exercises

Czechoslovakia	445.45
Hungary	440.55
United States	422.63

Modern Pentathlon

William Grut SWE	16
George Moore USA	47
Gösta Gärdin SWE	49

ROWING

Single Sculls

Mervyn Wood AUS	7:24.4
Eduardo Risso URU	7:38.2
Romolo Catasta ITA	7:51.4

Double Sculls

Richard Burnell & Bertie Bushnell GBR	6:51.3
Ebbe Parsner & Aage Larsen DEN	6:55.3
William Jones & Juan Rodríguez URU	7:12.4

Coxed Pairs

Finn Pedersen, Tage Henriksen & Carl-Ebbe Andersen DEN	8:00.5
Giovanni Steffe, Aldo Tarlao & Alberto Radi ITA	8:12.2
Antal Szendey, Béla Zsitnik & Róbert Zimonyi HUN	8:25.2

Coxless Pairs

John 'Jack' Wilson & William 'Ran' Laurie GBR	7:21.1
Hans Kalt & Josef Kalt SUI	7:23.9
Felice Fanetti & Bruno Boni ITA	7:31.5

Coxed Fours

United States	6:50.3
Switzerland	6:53.3
Denmark	6:58.6

Coxless Fours

Italy	6:39.0
Denmark	6:43.5
United States	6:47.7

Eights

United States	5:56.7
Great Britain	6:06.9
Norway	6:10.3

SAILING

6 Metres – 1919

United States	5472
Argentina	5120
Sweden	4033

Dragon

Thor Thorvaldsen, Sigve Lie & Håkon Barfod NOR	4746
Folke Bohlin, Hugo Jonsson & Gösta Brodin SWE	4621
William Berntsen, Ole Berntsen & Klaus Baess DEN	4223

Star

Hilary Smart & Paul Smart GBR	5828
Carlos de Cárdenas Sr & Carlos de Cárdenas Jr CUB	4949
Adriaan Maas & Edward Stutterheim NED	4731

Olympic Monotype

Paul Elvstrøm DEN	5543
Ralph Evans USA	5408
Jacobus de Jong NED	5204

Swallow

Stewart Morris & David Bond GBR	5625
Duarte de Almeida & Fernando Pinto Coelho POR	5579
Lockwood Pine & Owen Tory USA	4352

SHOOTING

Free Rifle Three Positions

Emil Grünig SUI	1120
Pauli Janhonen FIN	1114
Willy Røgeberg NOR	1112

Free Pistol

Edwin Vásquez PER	545
Rudolf Schnyder SUI	539
Torsten Ullman SWE	539

Rapid-Fire Pistol

Károly Takács HUN	580
Carlos Enrique Díaz Sáenz Valiente ARG	571
Sven Lundqvist SWE	569

Small Bore Rifle Prone

Arthur Cook USA	599
Walter Tomsen USA	599
Jonas Jonsson SWE	597

SWIMMING

Men's 100m Freestyle

Wally Ris USA	57.3
Alan Ford USA	57.8
Géza Kádas HUN	58.1

Men's 400m Freestyle

William Smith USA	4:41.0
Jimmy McLane USA	4:43.4
John Marshall AUS	4:47.4

Men's 1500m Freestyle

Jimmy McLane USA	19:18.5
John Marshall AUS	19:31.3
György Mitró HUN	19:43.2

Men's 100m Backstroke

Allen Stack USA	1:06.4
Robert Cowell USA	1:06.5
Georges Vallerey FRA	1:07.8

Men's 200m Breaststroke

Joseph Verdeur USA	2:39.3
Keith Carter USA	2:40.2
Robert Sohl USA	2:43.9

Men's 4 x 200m Relay

United States	8:46.0
Hungary	8:48.4
France	9:08.0

Women's 100m Freestyle

Greta Andersen DEN	1:06.3
Ann Curtis USA	1:06.5
Marie-Louise Vaessen NED	1:07.6

Women's 400m Freestyle

Ann Curtis USA	5:17.8
Karen Margrete Harup DEN	5:21.2
Catherine Gibson GBR	5:22.5

Women's 100m Backstroke

Karen Margrete Harup DEN	1:14.4
Suzanne Zimmerman USA	1:16.0
Judy-Joy Davies AUS	1:16.7

Women's 200m Breaststroke

Petronella van Vliet NED	2:57.2
Beatrice Lyons AUS	2:57.7
Éva Novák HUN	3:00.2

Women's 4 x 100m Relay

United States	4:29.2
Denmark	4:29.6
Netherlands	4:31.6

Water Polo

Italy	Gold
Hungary	Silver
Netherlands	Bronze

XIV Olympiad — Medallists

TRACK AND FIELD

Men's 100m

Harrison Dillard USA	10.3
Norwood 'Barney' Ewell USA	10.4
Lloyd LaBeach PAN	10.4

Men's 200m

Mel Patton USA	21.1
Norwood 'Barney' Ewell USA	21.1
Lloyd LaBeach PAN	21.2

Men's 400m

Arthur Wint JAM	46.2
Herb McKenley JAM	46.4
Mal Whitfield USA	46.9

Men's 800m

Mal Whitfield USA	1:49.2
Arthur Wint JAM	1:49.5
Marcel Hansenne FRA	1:49.8

Men's 1500m

Henry Eriksson SWE	3:49.8
Lennart Strand SWE	3:50.4
Willem Slijkhuis NED	3:50.4

Men's 5000m

Gaston Reiff BEL	14:17.6
Emil Zátopek TCH	14:17.8
Willem Slijkhuis NED	14:26.8

Men's 10,000m

Emil Zátopek TCH	29:59.6
Alain Mimoun FRA	30:47.4
Bertil Albertsson SWE	30:53.6

Men's Marathon

Delfo Cabrera ARG	2:34:52
Tom Richards GBR	2:35:08
Étienne Gailly BEL	2:35:54

Men's 110m Hurdles

Bill Porter USA	13.9
Clyde Scott USA	14.1
Craig Dixon USA	14.1

Men's 400m Hurdles

Roy Cochran USA	51.1
Duncan White CEY	51.8
Rune Larsson SWE	52.2

Men's 3000m Steeplechase

Tore Sjöstrand SWE	9:04.6
Erik Elmsäter SWE	9:08.2
Göte Hagström SWE	9:11.8

Men's 4 x 100m Relay

United States	40.6
Great Britain	41.3
Italy	41.5

Men's 4 x 400m Relay

United States	3:10.4
France	3:14.8
Sweden	3:16.0

Men's 10km Walk

John Mikaelsson SWE	45:13.2
Ingemar Johansson SWE	45:43.8
Fritz Schwab SUI	46:00.2

Men's 50km Walk

John Ljunggren SWE	4:41:52
Gaston Godel SUI	4:48:17
Tebbs Lloyd Johnson GBR	4:48:31

Men's Long Jump

Willie Steele USA	7.82m
Thomas Bruce AUS	7.55m
Herb Douglas USA	7.54m

Men's Triple Jump

Arne Åhman SWE	15.40m
George Avery AUS	15.365m
Ruhi Sarialp TUR	15.025m

Men's High Jump

John Winter AUS	1.98m
Bjørn Paulson NOR	1.95m
George Stanich USA	1.95m

Men's Pole Vault

Guinn Smith USA	4.30m
Erkki Kataja FIN	4.20m
Bob Richards USA	4.20m

Men's Shot Put

Wilbur Thompson USA	17.12m
Jim Delaney USA	16.68m
Jim Fuchs USA	16.42m

Men's Discus

Adolfo Consolini ITA	52.78m
Giuseppe Tosi ITA	51.78m
Fortune Gordien USA	50.77m

Men's Javelin

Tapio Rautavaara FIN	69.77m
Steve Seymour USA	67.56m
József Várszegi HUN	67.03m

Men's Hammer Throw

Imre Németh HUN	56.07m
Ivan Gubijan YUG	54.27m
Bob Bennett USA	53.73m

Men's Decathlon

Bob Mathias USA	7139m
Ignace Heinrich FRA	6974m
Floyd Simmons USA	6950m

Women's 100m

Fanny Blankers-Koen NED	11.9
Dorothy Manley GBR	12.2
Shirley Strickland AUS	12.2

Women's 200m

Fanny Blankers-Koen NED	24.4
Audrey Williamson GBR	25.1
Audrey Patterson USA	25.2

Women's 80m Hurdles

Fanny Blankers-Koen NED	11.2
Maureen Gardner GBR	11.2
Shirley Strickland AUS	11.3

Women's 4 x 100m Relay

Netherlands	47.5
Australia	47.6
Canada	47.8

Women's Long Jump

Olga Gyarmati HUN	5.695m
Noëmi de Portela ARG	5.60m
Ann-Britt Leyman SWE	5.575m

Women's High Jump

Alice Coachman USA	1.68m
Dorothy Tyler (Odam) GBR	1.68m
Micheline Ostermeyer FRA	1.61m

Women's Shot Put

Micheline Ostermeyer FRA	13.75m
Amelia Piccinini ITA	13.09m
Ina Schäffer AUT	13.08m

Women's Discus

Micheline Ostermeyer FRA	41.92m
Edera Gentile ITA	41.17m
Jacqueline Mazéas FRA	40.47m

Women's Javelin

Hermine Bauma AUT	45.57m
Kaisa Parviainen FIN	43.79m
Lily Carlstedt DEN	42.08m

WEIGHTLIFTING

Bantamweight

Joseph DePietro USA	307.5
Julian Creus GBR	297.5
Richard Tom USA	295.0

Featherweight

Mahmoud Fayad EGY	332.5
Rodney Wilkes TRI	317.5
Mohammad Jafar Salmassi IRN	312.5

Lightweight

Ibrahim Hassan Shams EGY	360.0
Attia Hamouda EGY	360.0
James Halliday GBR	340.0

Middleweight

Frank Spellman USA	390.0
Peter George USA	382.5
Kim Sung-Jip KOR	380.0

Light Heavyweight

Stanley Stanczyk USA	417.5
Harold Sakata USA	380.0
Gösta Magnusson SWE	375.0

Heavyweight

John Davis USA	452.5
Norbert Schemansky USA	425.0
Abraham Charité NED	412.5

WRESTLING – FREESTYLE

Flyweight

Lennart Viitala FIN	2
Halit Balamir TUR	2
Thure Johansson SWE	6

Bantamweight

Nasuh Akar TUR	0
Gerald Leeman USA	3
Charles Kouyos FRA	Bronze

Featherweight

Gazanfer Bilge TUR	1
Ivar Sjölin SWE	3
Adolf Müller SUI	Bronze

Lightweight

Celal Atik TUR	1
Gösta Frändfors SWE	6
Hermann Baumann SUI	8

Welterweight

Yasar Dogu TUR	1
Richard Garrard AUS	5
Leland Merrill USA	6

Middleweight

Glen Brand USA	0
Adil Candemir TUR	3
Erik Lindén SWE	Bronze

Light Heavyweight

Henry Wittenberg USA	2
Fritz Stöckli SUI	3
Bengt Fahlkvist SWE	

Heavyweight

Gyula Bóbis HUN	0
Bertil Antonsson SWE	2
Joseph Armstrong AUS	6

WRESTLING – GRECO-ROMAN

Flyweight	
Pietro Lombardi ITA	1
Kenan Olcay TUR	3
Reino Kangasmaki FIN	Bronze
Bantamweight	
Kurt Pettersén SWE	1
Ali Mahmoud Hassan EGY	3
Halil Kaya TUR	Bronze
Featherweight	
Mehmet Oktav TUR	0
Olle Anderberg SWE	3
Ferenc Tóth HUN	Bronze
Lightweight	
Gustav Freij SWE	Gold
Aage Eriksen NOR	Silver
Károly Ferencz HUN	1
Welterweight	
Gösta Andersson SWE	2
Miklós Szilvási HUN	3
Henrik Hansen DEN	6
Middleweight	
Axel Grönberg SWE	1
Muhlis Tayfur TUR	3
Ercole Gallegati ITA	Bronze
Light Heavyweight	
Karl-Erik Nilsson SWE	1
Kaelpo Gröndahl FIN	3
Ibrahim Orabi EGY	Bronze
Heavyweight	
Ahmet Kireççi TUR	1
Tor Nilsson SWE	3
Guido Fantoni ITA	6

LEADING MEDAL WINNERS

	G	S	B	T
MEN				
Veikko Huhtanen/Gymnastics FIN	3	1	1	**5**
Paavo Aaltonen/Gymnastics FIN	3	0	1	**4**
Jimmy McLane/Swimming USA	2	1	0	**3**
Humberto Mariles/Equestrian MEX	2	0	1	**3**
Mal Whitfield/Track USA	2	0	1	**3**
Barney Ewell/Track USA	1	2	0	**3**
Michael Reusch/Gymnastics SWI	1	2	0	**3**
Josef Stalder/Gymnastics SWI	1	1	1	**3**
Ferenc Pataki/Gymnastics HUN	1	0	2	**3**
Walter Lehmann/Gymnastics SWI	0	3	0	**3**
Edoardo Mangiarotti/Fencing ITA	0	2	1	**3**
János Mogyorósi/Gymnastics HUN	0	1	2	**3**
WOMEN				
Fanny Blankers-Koen/Track NED	4	0	0	**4**
Ann Curtis/Swimming USA	2	1	0	**3**
Micheline Ostermeyer/Track FRA	2	0	1	**3**
Karen-Margrete Harup/Swim DEN	1	2	0	**3**
Shirley Strickland/Track AUS	0	1	2	**3**

MEDALS BY NATION

	G	S	B
1 United States of America USA	38	27	19
2 Sweden SWE	16	11	17
3 France FRA	10	6	13
4 Hungary HUN	10	5	12
5 Italy ITA	8	11	8
6 Finland FIN	8	7	5
7 Turkey TUR	6	4	2
8 Czechoslovakia TCH	6	2	3
9 Switzerland SUI	5	10	5
10 Denmark DEN	5	7	8
11 Netherlands NED	5	2	9
12 Great Britain GBR	3	14	6
13 Argentina ARG	3	3	1
14 Australia AUS	3	3	1
15 Belgium BEL	2	2	3
16 Egypt EGY	2	2	1
17 Mexico MEX	2	1	2
18 South Africa RSA	2	1	1
19 Norway NOR	1	3	3
20 Jamaica JAM	1	2	0
21 Austria AUT	1	0	3
22 India IND	1	0	0
23 Peru PER	1	0	0
24 Yugoslavia YUG	0	2	0
25 Canada CAN	0	1	2
26 Uruguay URU	0	1	1
27 Portugal POR	0	1	1
28 Spain ESP	0	1	0
29 Sri Lanka SRI	0	1	0
30 Trinidad and Tobago TRI	0	1	0
31 Cuba CUB	0	1	0
32 Korea KOR	0	0	2
33 Panama PAN	0	0	2
34 Poland POL	0	0	1
35 Puerto Rico PUR	0	0	1
36 Islamic Republic of Iran IRI	0	0	1
37 Brazil BRA	0	0	1

Football — World Cup Finals

WORLD CUP FINALS

1966		
ENGLAND	0–0	URUGUAY
ENGLAND R Charlton 38, Hunt 74	2–0	MEXICO
ENGLAND Hunt 38, 75	2–0	FRANCE
Quarter-Final ENGLAND Hurst 78	1–0	ARGENTINA
Semi-Final ENGLAND R Charlton 30, 79	2–1	PORTUGAL Eusébio pen 82
Final ENGLAND Hurst 18, 102, 120, Peters 78	4–2 aet	WEST GERMANY Haller 12, Weber 90

WORLD CUP QUALIFYING

1957		
ENGLAND Taylor 8, 17, 40, Atyeo 38, 90	5–1	R OF IRELAND Curtis 56
1961		
ENGLAND Connelly 5, Pointer 9	2–0	PORTUGAL
1973		
ENGLAND Hunter 42	1–1	WALES Toshack 23
ENGLAND Clarke pen 63	1–1	POLAND Domarski 55
1976		
ENGLAND Tueart 4, Royle 52	2–1	FINLAND Nieminen 48
1977		
ENGLAND Keegan 10, Francis 58, Kennedy 65, Channon 69, 81 (pen)	5–0	LUXEMBOURG
ENGLAND Keegan 11, Brooking 80	2–0	ITALY
1980		
ENGLAND McDermott 37 (pen), 75, Woodcock 66, Mariner 85	4–0	NORWAY
ENGLAND Tanner og 22, Mariner 36	2–1	SWITZERLAND Pfister 76
1981		
ENGLAND	0–0	ROMANIA
ENGLAND Mariner 14	1–0	HUNGARY
1984		
ENGLAND Hateley 29, 49, Woodcock 40, Robson 70, Sansom 85	5–0	FINLAND

Football — European Championships

1985		
ENGLAND Hoddle 25	1–1	ROMANIA Camataru 60
ENGLAND Waddle 15, Lineker 18, 43, 54, Robson 35	5–0	TURKEY
ENGLAND	0–0	N IRELAND
1988		
ENGLAND	0–0	SWEDEN
1989		
ENGLAND Lineker 5, Beardsley 12, 64, Waddle 72, Gascoigne 88	5–0	ALBANIA
ENGLAND Lineker 24, Barnes 69, Webb 82	3–0	POLAND
1992		
ENGLAND Platt 55	1–1	NORWAY Rekdal 76
ENGLAND Gascoigne 16, 62, Shearer 28, Pearce 61	4–0	TURKEY
1993		
ENGLAND Platt 13, 24, 67, 83, Palmer 77, Ferdinand 86	6–0	SAN MARINO
ENGLAND Barnes 1, Platt 23	2–2	NETHERLANDS Bergkamp 34, Van Vossen pen 85
ENGLAND Ferdinand 5, Gascoigne 49, Pearce 53	3–0	POLAND
1996		
ENGLAND Shearer 24, 37	2–1	POLAND Citko 6
1997		
ENGLAND	0–1	ITALY Zola 18
ENGLAND Sheringham 42, Shearer 90	2–0	GEORGIA
ENGLAND Scholes 28, Wright 46, 90, Gascoigne 80	4–0	MOLDOVA
2000		
ENGLAND	0–1	GERMANY Hamann 14

EUROPEAN CHAMPIONSHIP FINALS

1968		
Quarter-Final (1st leg) ENGLAND R Charlton 84	1–0	SPAIN
1972		
Quarter-Final (1st leg) ENGLAND Lee 77	1–3	GERMANY Hoeness 26, Netzer pen 84, Muller 88
1996		
ENGLAND Shearer 22	1–1	SWITZERLAND Turkyilmaz pen 82
ENGLAND Shearer 52, Gascoigne 78	2–0	SCOTLAND
ENGLAND Shearer pen 22, 57, Sheringham 51, 62	4–1	NETHERLANDS Kluivert 77
Quarter-Final ENGLAND	0–0 aet (won 4-2 on pens)	SPAIN
Semi-Final ENGLAND Shearer 2	1–1 aet (lost 6-5 on pens)	GERMANY Kuntz 15
1999		
Play-off (2nd leg) ENGLAND	0–1	SCOTLAND Hutchinson 38

EUROPEAN CHAMPIONSHIP QUALIFYING

1966		
ENGLAND Hurst 30, 34, R Charlton 43 Hennessey og 80, J Charlton 84	5–1	WALES W Davies 38
1967		
ENGLAND Charlton (J) 84, Hurst 88	2–3	SCOTLAND Law 27, Lennox 78, McCalliog 87
ENGLAND Hurst 44, Charlton 62	2–0	N IRELAND
1971		
ENGLAND Chivers 23, Hurst 68, Lee 87	3–0	GREECE
ENGLAND Chivers 30, 48, Lee 43, Clarke pen 46, Lawler 75	5–0	MALTA
ENGLAND Summerbee 9	1–1	SWITZERLAND Odermatt 26
1974		
ENGLAND Channon 72, Bell 80, 83	3–0	CZECHOSLOVAKIA
ENGLAND	0–0	PORTUGAL
1975		
ENGLAND Macdonald 2, 35, 48, 53, 88	5–0	CYPRUS
1979		
ENGLAND Keegan 25, Latchford 46, 63, Watson 49	4–0	N IRELAND
ENGLAND Keegan 18	1–0	DENMARK
ENGLAND Watson 9, Hoddle 68	2–0	BULGARIA
1980		
ENGLAND Keegan 35, 75	2–0	R OF IRELAND
1982		
ENGLAND Moes og 18, Coppell 21, Woodcock 34, Blissett 43, 62, 86, Chamberlain 72, Hoddle 88, Neal 90	9–0	LUXEMBOURG

Football — Internationals

1983			
ENGLAND	0–0	GREECE	
ENGLAND Francis 30, With 70	2–0	HUNGARY	
ENGLAND	0–1	DENMARK Simonsen pen 39	
1986			
ENGLAND Lineker 33, 80, Waddle 78	3–0	N IRELAND	
ENGLAND Mabbutt 21, Anderson 57	2–0	YUGOSLAVIA	
1987			
ENGLAND Barnes 2, 28, Lineker 8, 42, 71, Robson 59, Beardsley 62, Webb 88	8–0	TURKEY	
1990			
ENGLAND Lineker pen 39, Beardsley 89	2–0	POLAND	
1991			
ENGLAND Dixon 9	1–1	R OF IRELAND Quinn 28	
ENGLAND Smith 21	1–0	TURKEY	
1998			
ENGLAND	0–0	BULGARIA	
1999			
ENGLAND Scholes 11, 21, 70	3–1	POLAND Brzeczek 28	
ENGLAND	0–0	SWEDEN	
ENGLAND Shearer pen 12, 28, 34, McManaman 30, 44, Owen 90	6–0	LUXEMBOURG	
INTERNATIONALS			
1941			
ENGLAND Welsh 16, Hagan 35	2–0	SCOTLAND	
BELGIUM De Busscher 2, Schuermans, Landrieux, Clerinckx	5–4	NETHERLANDS Luttmer, Van Elsacker, Van der Gender 2	
1942			
ENGLAND Hagan 1, Lawton 53, 65	3–0	SCOTLAND	
ENGLAND	0–0	SCOTLAND	
1943			
ENGLAND Carter (2), Westcott (3)	5–3	WALES Lowrie (3)	
ENGLAND Carter (2), Welsh (3), Hagan (2), Compton	8–3	WALES Lowrie (2), A Powell	
1944			
ENGLAND Hagan (2), Macaulay og, Lawton, Mercer, Carter	6–2	SCOTLAND Dodds (2)	
ENGLAND Lawton (3), Goulden, Carter, Smith	6–2	SCOTLAND Milne, Walker	
1945			
ENGLAND Carter 10, Lawton 79	2–2	FRANCE Vaast 44, Heisserer 90	
1946			
VICTORY INTERNATIONAL ENGLAND	2–0	BELGIUM	
1951			
ENGLAND Mortensen 79, Milburn 86	2–1	ARGENTINA Boye 18	
ENGLAND Ramsay pen 68, Lofthouse 75	2–2	AUSTRIA Melchior 47, Stojaspol pen 87	
1952			
ENGLAND Elliott 4, 48, Lofthouse 42, 86, R Froggatt 60	5–0	BELGIUM	
1953			
ENGLAND Sewell 13, Mortensen 38, Ramsay pen 57	3–6	HUNGARY Hidegkuti 1, 20, 53, Puskás 24, 29, Bozsik 50	
1954			
ENGLAND Bentley 28, Allen 48, Shackleton 80	3–1	WEST GERMANY Beck 75	
1955			
ENGLAND Atyeo 12, Perry 13, 60, Finney 59	4–1	SPAIN Arieta 80	
1956			
ENGLAND Taylor 3, 65, Grainger 5, 84	4–2	BRAZIL Paulinho 53, Didi 55	
ENGLAND Brooks 13, Taylor 65, 89	3–0	YUGOSLAVIA	
1957			
ENGLAND Taylor 3, 33, Robson 24, 84	4–0	FRANCE	
1958			
ENGLAND Charlton 24, 60	2–1	PORTUGAL Duarte 50	
ENGLAND Haynes 45, 63, 82, Charlton pen 84, Lofthouse 90	5–0	USSR	
1959			
ENGLAND Charlton 26, Bradley 38	2–2	ITALY Brighenti 56, Mariani 61	
ENGLAND Connolly 9, Charlton 81	2–3	SWEDEN Simonsson 52, 60, Salomonsson 75	
1960			
ENGLAND Douglas 44, Greaves 48, Haynes 88	3–3	YUGOSLAVIA Galic 31, 60, Kostic 80	
ENGLAND Greaves 1, Douglas 41, Smith 68, 79	4–2	SPAIN Del Sol 14, Suarez 51	
1961			
ENGLAND Hitchens 2, Charlton 12, 62, 73, Robson 23, Douglas 44, 85 Flowers pen 59	8–0	MEXICO	
1962			
ENGLAND Crawford 8, Flowers pen 38, Hunt 67	3–1	AUSTRIA Buzek 79	
ENGLAND Flowers 20, Hitchens 21, Connelly 36	3–1	SWITZERLAND Allemann 32	
1963			
ENGLAND Douglas 86	1–1	BRAZIL Pepe 18	
1964			
ENGLAND Byrne 43, 52	2–1	URUGUAY Spencer 78	
ENGLAND Pickering 32, Hinton 70	2–2	BELGIUM Cornelis 22, Van Himst 42	
1965			
ENGLAND Greaves 17	1–0	HUNGARY	
ENGLAND R Charlton 3, Connelly 59	2–3	AUSTRIA Flogel 53, Fritsch 73, 81	
1966			
ENGLAND Stiles 41	1–0	WEST GERMANY	
ENGLAND Greaves 9, R Charlton 34	2–0	YUGOSLAVIA	
ENGLAND	0–0	CZECHOSLOVAKIA	
1967			
ENGLAND Greaves 70, Hunt 75	2–0	SPAIN	
ENGLAND Ball 23, Peters 72	2–2	USSR Chislenko 42, 44	
1968			
ENGLAND Peters 36, Charlton 38, Hunt 72	3–1	SWEDEN Andersson 90	
ENGLAND Hurst 36	1–1	BULGARIA Asparoukhov 32	
1969			
ENGLAND J Charlton 27	1–1	ROMANIA Dumitrache pen 74	
ENGLAND O'Grady 33, Hurst pen 48, 49, pen 80 Lee 75	5–0	FRANCE	
ENGLAND J Charlton 24	1–0	PORTUGAL	
1970			
ENGLAND	0–0	NETHERLANDS	
ENGLAND Lee 12, Peters 21, Clarke 63	3–1	EAST GERMANY Vogel 27	
1972			
ENGLAND Royle 40	1–1	YUGOSLAVIA Vladic 50	
1973			
ENGLAND Channon 8, 48, Clarke 28, 43, Chivers 61,Currie 64, Bell 87	7–0	AUSTRIA	
ENGLAND	0–1	ITALY Capello 86	

Football — Internationals

1974	ENGLAND Channon 44, Worthington 53	2–2	ARGENTINA Kempes 57, pen 89
1975	ENGLAND Bell 25, Macdonald 66	2–0	WEST GERMANY
1976	ENGLAND Pearson 45	1–1	R OF IRELAND Daly pen 52
1977	ENGLAND	0–2	NETHERLANDS Peters 29, 38
	ENGLAND	0–0	SWITZERLAND
1978	ENGLAND Keegan 70	1–1	BRAZIL Gil 9
	ENGLAND Coppell 69	1–0	CZECHOSLOVAKIA
1980	ENGLAND Johnson 42, 50, Keegan 69	3–1	ARGENTINA Passarella pen 55
1981	ENGLAND Hoddle 26	1–2	SPAIN Satrustegui 6, Zamora 32
	ENGLAND	0–1	BRAZIL Zico 12
1982	ENGLAND Woodcock 48, Mariner 53	2–0	NETHERLANDS
	ENGLAND Woodcock 85	1–2	WEST GERMANY Rummenigge 73, 82
1984	ENGLAND	0–2	USSR Gotsmanov 53, Protasov 90
	ENGLAND Robson 82	1–0	EAST GERMANY
1985	ENGLAND Steven 45, Lineker 76	2–1	R OF IRELAND Brady 88
1988	ENGLAND Lineker 13, Adams 61	2–2	NETHERLANDS Adams og 20, Bosman 25
	ENGLAND Webb 28	1–0	DENMARK
1989	ENGLAND	0–0	ITALY
	ENGLAND Robson 1, 70	2–1	YUGOSLAVIA Skoro 17
1990	ENGLAND Lineker 36	1–0	BRAZIL
	ENGLAND Bull 18, 55, Pearce 23, Gascoigne 89	4–2	CZECHOSLOVAKIA Skuhravy 10, Kubik 81
	ENGLAND Lineker 54	1–0	DENMARK
	ENGLAND Barnes 50	1–2	URUGUAY Ostolaza 26, Perdomo 61
	ENGLAND Lineker 44	1–0	HUNGARY
1991	ENGLAND Lineker pen 20, 60	2–0	CAMEROON
	ENGLAND Smith 16, Platt pen 43, 89	3–1	USSR M Wright og 9
	ENGLAND Lineker 15, Platt 50	2–2	ARGENTINA Garcia 66, Franco 70
	ENGLAND	0–1	GERMANY Riedle 45
1992	ENGLAND Shearer 44, Lineker 73	2–0	FRANCE
	ENGLAND Platt 49	1–1	BRAZIL Bebeto 25
1994	ENGLAND Platt 16	1–0	DENMARK
	ENGLAND Anderton 23, Beardsley 37, Platt pen 44, 55, Shearer 65	5–0	GREECE
	ENGLAND	0–0	NORWAY
	ENGLAND Shearer 33, 40	2–0	USA
	ENGLAND Lee 45	1–1	ROMANIA Dumitrescu 36
	ENGLAND Platt 41	1–0	NIGERIA
1995 UMBRO CUP	ENGLAND Anderton 48, Platt pen 88	2–1	JAPAN Ihara 62
	ENGLAND Le Saux 38	1–3	BRAZIL Juninho 54, Ronaldo 61, Edmundo 76
1995	ENGLAND	0–0	URUGUAY
	ENGLAND	0–0	COLOMBIA
	ENGLAND Pearce 45, Sheringham 56, Stone 78	3–1	SWITZERLAND Knup 41
	ENGLAND Stone 44	1–1	PORTUGAL Alves 58
1996	ENGLAND Ferdinand 7	1–0	BULGARIA
	ENGLAND	0–0	CROATIA
	ENGLAND Anderton 38, 62, Platt 52	3–0	HUNGARY
1997	ENGLAND Sheringham pen 19, Fowler 56	2–0	MEXICO
	ENGLAND Scholes 44, Fowler 45	2–0	CAMEROON
1998	ENGLAND	0–2	CHILE Salas 45, pen 79
	ENGLAND Shearer 5, 65, Sheringham 46	3–0	PORTUGAL
	ENGLAND	0–0	SAUDI ARABIA
	ENGLAND Anderton 22, Merson 39	2–0	CZECH REPUBLIC
1999	ENGLAND	0–2	FRANCE Anelka 69, 76
2000	ENGLAND	0–0	ARGENTINA
	ENGLAND Owen 38	1–1	BRAZIL Franca 44
	ENGLAND Fowler 44, Adams 67	2–0	UKRAINE

Football — European Finals

EUROPEAN CUP FINALS

1963	BENFICA Eusébio 18	1–2	AC MILAN Altafini 58, 70
1968	BENFICA Graca 81	1–4 aet	MANCHESTER UTD Charlton 52, 98, Best 92, Kidd 97
1971	AJAX AMSTERDAM Van Dijk 5, Kapsis og 87	2–0	PANATHINAIKOS
1978	BRUGES	0–1	LIVERPOOL Daglish 66
1992	BARCELONA Koeman 111	1–0 aet	SAMPDORIA

EUROPEAN CUP-WINNERS' CUP FINALS

1965	TSV MUNICH	0–2	WEST HAM UTD Sealey 69, 71
1993	PARMA Minotti 9, Melli 30, Cuoghi 84	3–1	ROYAL ANTWERP Severeyns 11

Football —
FA Cup Finals

FA CUP FINALS

1923	BOLTON W Jack 3, JR Smith 54	2–0	WEST HAM UTD
1924	ASTON VILLA Harris 83, Seymour 85	0–2	NEWCASTLE UTD
1925	CARDIFF CITY	0–1	SHEFFIELD UNITED Tunstall 30
1926	BOLTON W Jack 76	1–0	MANCHESTER CITY
1927	ARSENAL	0–1	CARDIFF CITY Ferguson 74
1928	BLACKBURN R Roscamp 1, 85, McLean 22	3–1	HUDDERSFIELD T Jackson 55
1929	BOLTON W Butler 79, Blackmore 87	2–0	PORTSMOUTH
1930	ARSENAL James 16, Lambert 88	2–0	HUDDERSFIELD TOWN
1931	BIRMINGHAM Bradford 57	1–2	WEST BROMWICH A W G Richardson 25, 58
1932	ARSENAL John 15	1–2	NEWCASTLE UTD Allen 38, 72
1933	EVERTON Stein 41, Dean 52, Dunn 80	3–0	MANCHESTER CITY
1934	MANCHESTER CITY Tilson 73, 87	2–1	PORTSMOUTH Rutherford 26
1935	SHEFFIELD WED Palethorpe 2, Hooper 70, Rimmer 85, 89	4–2	WEST BROMWICH A Boyes 21, Sandford 75
1936	ARSENAL Drake 75	1–0	SHEFFIELD UTD
1937	PRESTON N E F O'Donnell 44	1–3	SUNDERLAND Gurney 52, Carter 70, Burbanks 87
1938	HUDDERSFIELD T	0–1	PRESTON N E Mutch pen, 120
1939	PORTSMOUTH Barlow 29, Anderson 43, Parker 46, 71	4–1	WOLVERHAMPTON W Dorsett 54
1946	CHARLTON ATH H Turner 86	1–4	DERBY COUNTY H Turner og 85, Doherty 92, Stamps 97, 106
1947	BURNLEY	0–1	CHARLTON A Duffy 114
1948	BLACKPOOL Shimwell pen 12, Mortensen 35	2–4	MANCHESTER UTD Rowley 28, 70, Pearson 80, Anderson 82
1949	LEICESTER CITY Griffiths 46	1–3	WOLVERHAMPTON W Pye 13, 42, Smyth 68
1950	ARSENAL Lewis 18, 63	2–0	LIVERPOOL
1951	BLACKPOOL	0–2	NEWCASTLE UTD Milburn 50, 55
1952	ARSENAL	0–1	NEWCASTLE UTD G Robledo 84
1953	BLACKPOOL Mortensen 35, 68, 89, Perry 90	4–3	BOLTON W Lofthouse 2, Moir 39, Bell 55
1954	PRESTON N E Morrison 22, Wayman 51	2–3	WEST BROMWICH A Allen 21, 63 pen, Griffin 87
1955	MANCHESTER CITY Johnstone 44	1–3	NEWCASTLE UNITED Milburn 1, Mitchell 53, Hannah 60
1956	BIRMINGHAM CITY Kinsey 1	1–3	MANCHESTER CITY Hayes 3, Dyson 65, Johnstone 68
1957	ASTON VILLA McParland 68, 73	2–1	MANCHESTER UTD Taylor 83
1958	BOLTON W Lofthouse 3, 50	2–0	MANCHESTER UTD
1959	LUTON TOWN Pacey 62	1–2	NOTTINGHAM F Dwight 10, Wilson 14
1960	BLACKBURN R	0–3	WOLVERHAMPTON W McGrath og 41, Deeley 67, 88
1961	LEICESTER CITY	0–2	TOTTENHAM H Smith 70, Dyson 77
1962	BURNLEY Robson 50	1–3	TOTTENHAM H Greaves 3, Smith 51, Blanchflower pen 80
1963	LEICESTER CITY Keyworth 80	1–3	MANCHESTER UTD Law 30, Herd 57, 85
1964	PRESTON N E Holden 9, Dawson 40	2–3	WEST HAM UTD Sissons 10, Hurst 52, Boyce 90
1965	LEEDS Bremner 95	1–2 aet	LIVERPOOL Hunt 93, St John 113
1966	EVERTON Trebilcock 59, 64, Temple 80	3–2	SHEFFIELD WED McCalliog 3, Ford 57
1967	CHELSEA Tambling 85	1–2	TOTTENHAM H Robertson 40, Saul 67
1968	EVERTON	0–1	WEST BROMWICH A Astle 93
1969	LEICESTER CITY	0–1	MANCHESTER CITY Young 24
1970	CHELSEA Houseman 41, Hutchinson 86	2–2	LEEDS UTD Charlton 21, Jones 84
	CHELSEA Osgood 78, Webb 104	2–1 aet Replay (Old Trafford)	LEEDS UTD Jones 35
1971	ARSENAL Kelly 101, George 111	2–1	LIVERPOOL Heighway 91
1972	ARSENAL	0–1	LEEDS UTD Clarke 53
1973	LEEDS UTD	0–1	SUNDERLAND Porterfield 32
1974	LIVERPOOL Keegan 57, 88, Heighway 74	3–0	NEWCASTLE UTD
1975	FULHAM	0–2	WEST HAM UTD A Taylor 60, 64
1976	MANCHESTER UTD	0–1	SOUTHAMPTON Stokes 83
1977	LIVERPOOL Case 53	1–2	MANCHESTER UTD Pearson 51, J Greenhoff 55
1978	ARSENAL	0–1	IPSWICH TOWN Osborne 77
1979	ARSENAL Talbot 12, Stapleton 43, Sunderland 89	3–2	MANCHESTER UTD McQueen 86, McIlroy 88
1980	ARSENAL	0–1	WEST HAM UTD Brooking 13
1981	MANCHESTER CITY Hutchison 30	1–1	TOTTENHAM H Hutchison og 80
	MANCHESTER CITY Mackenzie 11, Reeves pen 50	2–3 Replay	TOTTENHAM H Villa 8, 77, Crooks 70
1982	QUEENS PARK R Fenwick 115	1–1	TOTTENHAM H Hoddle 109
	QUEENS PARK R	0–1 Replay	TOTTENHAM H Hoddle pen 6

Football — FA Cup Finals

1983	BRIGHTON & HOVE (Smith 14, Stevens 87)	2–2	MANCHESTER UTD (Stapleton 55, Wilkins 72)
	BRIGHTON & HOVE	0–4 Replay	MANCHESTER UTD (Robson 25, 44, Whiteside 30, Muhren pen 62)
1984	EVERTON (Sharp 38, Gray 51)	2–0	WATFORD
1985	EVERTON	0–1	MANCHESTER UTD (Whiteside 110)
1986	EVERTON (Lineker 28)	1–3	LIVERPOOL (Rush 57, 84, Johnston 63)
1987	COVENTRY CITY (Bennett 9, Houchen 63, Mabbutt og 96)	3–2	TOTTENHAM H (C Allen 2, Kilcline og 40)
1988	LIVERPOOL	0–1	WIMBLEDON (Sanchez 36)
1989	EVERTON (McCall 89, 102)	2–3 aet	LIVERPOOL (Aldridge 4, Rush 94, 104)
1990	CRYSTAL PALACE (O'Reilly 18, Wright 69, 91)	3–3 aet	MANCHESTER UTD (Robson 35, Hughes 61, 112)
	CRYSTAL PALACE	0–1 Replay	MANCHESTER UTD (Martin 59)
1991	NOTTINGHAM F (Pearce 15)	1–2	TOTTENHAM H (Stewart 53, Walker og 94)
1992	LIVERPOOL (Thomas 47, Rush 68)	2–0	SUNDERLAND
1993	ARSENAL (Wright 20)	1–1	SHEFFIELD WED (Hirst 61)
	ARSENAL (Wright 34, Linighan 119)	2–1 aet Replay	SHEFFIELD WED (Waddle 68)
1994	CHELSEA	0–4	MANCHESTER UTD (Cantona pens 60, 66, Hughes 69, McClair 90)
1995	EVERTON (Rideout 30)	1–0	MANCHESTER UTD
1996	LIVERPOOL	0–1	MANCHESTER UTD (Cantona 85)
1997	CHELSEA (Di Matteo 1, Newton 82)	2–0	MIDDLESBROUGH
1998	ARSENAL (Overmars 23, Anelka 69)	2–0	NEWCASTLE UNITED
1999	MANCHESTER UTD (Sheringham 11, Scholes 53)	2–0	NEWCASTLE UTD
2000	ASTON VILLA	0–1	CHELSEA (Di Matteo 72)

WAR-TIME CUP FINALS

1940	BLACKBURN R	0–1	WEST HAM UTD (Small 36)
1941	ARSENAL (D Compton 40)	1–1	PRESTON N E (McLaren 10)
	ARSENAL (Gallimore og)	1–2	PRESTON N E (R Beattie 2)
	Replay (Ewood Park, Blackburn)		

LONDON WAR CUP FINAL

1942	BRENTFORD (Smith 11, 90)	2–0	PORTSMOUTH

FOOTBALL LEAGUE SOUTH CUP FINALS

1943	ARSENAL (Lewis 4, 19, 51, 74, D Compton 8, Drake 26, 47)	7–1	CHARLTON A (Green pen 13)
1944	CHARLTON A (Revell 13, 35, Welsh 35)	3–1	CHELSEA (Payne pen 11)
1945	CHELSEA (McDonald 47, Wardle 52)	2–0	MILLWALL

FA CUP SEMI-FINALS

1991	ARSENAL (Smith 44)	1–3	TOTTENHAM H (Gascoigne 5, Lineker 11, 75)
1993	SHEFFIELD UTD (Cork 43)	1–2 aet	SHEFFIELD WED (Waddle 1, Bright 106)
	ARSENAL (Adams 79)	1–0	TOTTENHAM H
1994	CHELSEA (Peacock 13, 47)	2–0	LUTON TOWN
1994	MANCHESTER UTD (Hughes 119)	1–1	OLDHAM A (Pointon 106)
	MANCHESTER UTD (Irwin, Kanchelskis, Robson, Giggs)	4–1	OLDHAM A (Pointon)
	Replay (Maine Road, Manchester)		
2000	ASTON VILLA	0–0 aet	BOLTON W
	Aston Villa won 4–1 on penalties		
	CHELSEA (Poyet 17, 72)	2–1	NEWCASTLE UTD (Lee 66)

Football — FA Charity Shield

FA CHARITY SHIELD

1974	LEEDS UTD (Cherry 70)	1–1	LIVERPOOL (Boersma 19)
	Liverpool won 6–5 on penalties		
1975	DERBY COUNTY (Hector 19, McFarland 42)	2–0	WEST HAM UTD
1976	LIVERPOOL (Toshack 50)	1–0	SOUTHAMPTON
1977	LIVERPOOL	0–0 (shared shield)	MANCHESTER UTD
1978	IPSWICH TOWN	0–5	NOTTINGHAM FOR (O'Neill 10, 76, Withe 27, Lloyd 47, Robertson 88)
1979	ARSENAL (Sunderland 86)	1–3	LIVERPOOL (McDermott 39, 67, Dalglish 64)
1980	LIVERPOOL (McDermott 17)	1–0	WEST HAM UTD
1981	ASTON VILLA (Withe 30, 52)	2–2	TOTTENHAM (Falco 43, 47)
1982	LIVERPOOL (Rush 33)	1–0	TOTTENHAM
1983	LIVERPOOL	0–2	MANCHESTER UTD (Robson 23, 61)
1984	EVERTON (Grobbelaar og 55)	1–0	LIVERPOOL
1985	EVERTON (Steven 26, Heath 82)	2–0	MANCHESTER UTD
1986	EVERTON (Heath 80)	1–1	LIVERPOOL (Rush 89)
1987	COVENTRY CITY	0–1	EVERTON (Clarke 44)
1988	LIVERPOOL (Aldridge 23, 68)	2–1	WIMBLEDON (Fashanu 17)
1989	ARSENAL	0–1	LIVERPOOL (Beardsley 32)
1990	LIVERPOOL (Barnes pen 51)	1–1	MANCHESTER UTD (Blackmore 45)
1991	ARSENAL	0–0	TOTTENHAM
1992	LEEDS UTD (Cantona 25, 77, 87, Dorigo 43)	4–3	LIVERPOOL (Rush 34, Saunders 65, Strachan og 89)

Football — League Cup Finals

1993		
ARSENAL Wright 44	1–1	MANCHESTER UTD Hughes 8
	Manchester United won 5–4 on penalties	
1994		
BLACKBURN R	0–2	MANCHESTER UTD Cantona pen 21, Ince 80
1995		
BLACKBURN R	0–1	EVERTON Samways 58
1996		
MANCHESTER UTD Cantona 25, Butt 30, Beckham 86, Keane 88	4–0	NEWCASTLE UTD
1997		
CHELSEA Hughes 52	1–1	MANCHESTER UTD Johnsen 57
	Manchester United won 4–2 on penalties	
1998		
ARSENAL Overmars 33, Wreh 56, Anelka 71	3–0	MANCHESTER UTD
1999		
ARSENAL Kanu pen 67, Parlour 77	2–1	MANCHESTER UTD Beckham 36
2000		
CHELSEA Hasselbaink 22, Melchiot 72	2–0	MANCHESTER UTD

LEAGUE CUP FINALS

1967		
QUEENS PARK R Morgan 64, Marsh 75, Lazarus 82	3–2	WEST BROMWICH A Clark 7, 36
1968		
ARSENAL	0–1	LEEDS UTD Cooper 20
1969		
ARSENAL Gould 86	1–3 aet	SWINDON TOWN Smart 36, Rogers 105, 120
1970		
MANCHESTER CITY Doyle 59, Pardoe 102	2–1 aet	WEST BROMWICH A Astle 6
1971		
ASTON VILLA	0–2	TOTTENHAM H Chivers 77, 80
1972		
CHELSEA Osgood 45	1–2	STOKE CITY Conroy 4, Eastham 74
1973		
NORWICH CITY	0–1	TOTTENHAM H Coates 72
1974		
MANCHESTER CITY Bell 60	1–2	WOLVERHAMPTON W Hibbitt 43, Richards 85
1975		
ASTON VILLA Graydon 80	1–0	NORWICH CITY
1976		
MANCHESTER CITY Barnes 12, Tueart 46	2–1	NEWCASTLE UNITED Gowling 36
1977		
ASTON VILLA	0–0	EVERTON
ASTON VILLA Kenyon og 79	1–1 aet	EVERTON Latchford 88
	Replay (Hillsborough)	
ASTON VILLA Nicholl 80, Little 81, 120	3–2 aet	EVERTON Latchford 37, Lyons 83
	Replay (Old Trafford)	
1978		
LIVERPOOL	0–0 aet	NOTTINGHAM F
LIVERPOOL	0–1	NOTTINGHAM F Robertson 54 (pen)
	Replay (Old Trafford)	
1979		
NOTTINGHAM F Birtles 50, 78, Woodcock 82	3–2	SOUTHAMPTON Peach 16, Holmes 87
1980		
NOTTINGHAM F	0–1	WOLVERHAMPTON W Gray 67
1981		
LIVERPOOL A Kennedy 117	1–1 aet	WEST HAM UTD Stewart pen 120
LIVERPOOL Dalglish 26, Hansen 29	2–1	WEST HAM UNITED Goddard 10
	Replay (Villa Park)	
1982		
LIVERPOOL Whelan 87, 111, Rush 120	3–1 aet	TOTTENHAM H Archibald 11
1983		
LIVERPOOL Kennedy 75, Whelan 99	2–1 aet	MANCHESTER UNITED Whiteside 13
1984		
EVERTON	0–0 aet	LIVERPOOL
EVERTON	0–1	LIVERPOOL Souness 21
	Replay (Maine Road)	
1985		
NORWICH CITY Chisholm og 46	1–0	SUNDERLAND
1986		
OXFORD UNITED Hebberd 39, Houghton 52, Charles 86	3–0	QUEENS PARK R
1987		
ARSENAL Nicholas 28, 83	2–1	LIVERPOOL Rush 22
1988		
ARSENAL Hayes 71, Smith 74	2–3	LUTON TOWN B Stein 13, 90, Wilson 81
1989		
LUTON TOWN Harford 36	1–3	NOTTINGHAM FOREST Clough (pen) 55, 76, Web 67
1990		
NOTTINGHAM FOREST Jemson 48	1–0	OLDHAM ATHLETIC

Football — League Play-offs

1991		
MANCHESTER UTD	0–1	SHEFFIELD WED Sheridan 38
1992		
MANCHESTER UTD	1–0	NOTTINGHAM F McClair 13
1993		
ARSENAL Merson 18, Morrow 68	2–1	SHEFFIELD WED Harkes 9
1994		
ASTON VILLA Atkinson 25, Saunders 75, (pen) 89	3–1	MANCHESTER UTD Hughes 83
1995		
BOLTON W Thompson 69	1–2	LIVERPOOL McManaman 37, 68
1996		
ASTON VILLA Milosevic 20, Taylor 54, Yorke 89	3–0	LEEDS UNITED
1997		
LEICESTER CITY Heskey 118	1–1 aet	MIDDLESBROUGH Ravanelli 95
LEICESTER CITY Claridge	1–0	MIDDLESBROUGH
	Replay (Hillsborcugh)	
1998		
CHELSEA Sinclair 95, Di Matteo 107	2–0 aet	MIDDLESBROUGH
1999		
LEICESTER CITY	0–1	TOTTENHAM H Nielsen 90
2000		
LEICESTER CITY Elliott 29, 81	2–1	TRANMERE R Kelly 77

LEAGUE PLAY-OFF FINALS

1990		
2nd Division		
SUNDERLAND	0–1	SWINDON TOWN McLoughlin 27
3rd Division		
NOTTS COUNTY Johnson 31, Short 62	2–0	TRANMERE ROVERS
4th Division		
CAMBRIDGE UNITED Dublin 77	1–0	CHESTERFIELD
1991		
2nd Division		
BRIGHTON & HOVE Wilkins 89	1–3	NOTTS COUNTY Johnson 29, 59, Regis 71
3rd Division		
BOLTON W Malkin 97	0–1	TRANMERE ROVERS
4th Division		
BLACKPOOL Groves 6, Curran og 68	2–2	TORQUAY UNITED Saunders 28, Edwards pen 37
	Torquay United won 5–4 on penalties	

Football — League Play-offs

1992

2nd Division

BLACKBURN ROVERS Newell pen 45	1–0	LEICESTER CITY

3rd Division

PETERBOROUGH UTD Charlery 52, 89	2–1	STOCKPORT COUNTY

4th Division

BLACKPOOL Bamber 41	1–1	SCUNTHORPE UTD Daws 53

Blackpool won 4–3 on penalties

1993

1st Division

LEICESTER CITY Joachim 56, Walsh 68, 69	3–4	SWINDON TOWN Hoddle 41, Maskell 47, Thompson Taylor 53, Bodin pen 84

2nd Division

PORT VALE	0–3	WEST BROMWICH A Hunt 66, Reid 82, Donovan 90

3rd Division

CREWE ALEXANDRA McKearney pen 119	1–1 aet	YORK CITY Swann 104

York City won 5–3 on penalties

1994

1st Division

DERBY COUNTY Johnson 27	1–2	LEICESTER CITY Walsh 40, 86

2nd Division

BURNLEY Eyres 28, Parkinson 65	2–1	STOCKPORT COUNTY Beaumont 2

3rd Division

PRESTON N E Bryson 32, Raynor 37	2–4	WYCOMBE W Thompson 33, Garner 47, Carroll 57, 72

1995

1st Division

BOLTON WANDERERS Coyle 75, De Freitas 86, 118, Paatelainen 105	4–3	READING Nogan 4, Williams 12, Quinn 119

2nd Division

BRISTOL ROVERS Stewart 45	1–2	HUDDERSFIELD T Booth 44, Billy 81

3rd Division

BURY	0–2	CHESTERFIELD Lormor 23, Robinson 41

1996

1st Division

CRYSTAL PALACE Roberts 14	1–2 aet	LEICESTER CITY Parken pen 76, Claridge 120

2nd Division

BRADFORD CITY Hamilton 8, Stallard 73	2–0	NOTTS COUNTY

3rd Division

DARLINGTON	0–1	PLYMOUTH ARGYLE Mauge 65

1997

1st Division

CRYSTAL PALACE Hopkin 89	1–0	SHEFFIELD UNITED

2nd Division

BRENTFORD	0–1	CREWE ALEXANDRA Smith 34

3rd Division

NORTHAMPTON TOWN Frain 90	1–0	SWANSEA CITY

1998

1st Division

CHARLTON ATHLETIC Mendonca 23, 71, 103, Rufus 85	4–4 aet	SUNDERLAND Quinn 50, 73, Phillips 58, Summerbee 99

Charlton Athletic won
7–6 on penalties

2nd Division

GRIMSBY TOWN Donovan 19	1–0	NORTHAMPTON T

1999

1st Division

BOLTON W	0–2	WATFORD Wright 38, Smart 89

2nd Division

GILLINGHAM Asaba 81, Taylor 86	2–2 aet	MANCHESTER CITY Horlock 89, Dickov 90

Manchester City won
3–1 on penalties

3rd Division

LEYTON ORIENT	0–1	SCUNTHORPE UNITED Calvo-Garcia 6

2000

1st Division

BARNSLEY R Wright og 6, Hignett pen 78	2–4	IPSWICH TOWN Mowbray 28, Naylor 52, Stewart 58, Reuser 90

2nd Division

GILLINGHAM McGibbon og 35, Butler 114, Thomson 118	3–2 aet	WIGAN ATHLETIC Haworth 52, Barlow pen 99

3rd Division

DARLINGTON	0–1	PETERBOROUGH UTD Clarke 74

Rugby League — Challenge Cup Finals

CHALLENGE CUP FINALS

1929	WIGAN	13–2	DEWSBURY
1930	WIDNES	10–3	ST HELENS
1931	HALIFAX	22–8	YORK
1933	HUDDERSFIELD	21–17	WARRINGTON
1934	HUNSLET	11–5	WIDNES
1935	CASTLEFORD	11–8	HUDDERSFIELD
1936	LEEDS	18–2	WARRINGTON
1937	WIDNES	18–5	KEIGHLEY
1938	SALFORD	7–4	BARROW
1939	HALIFAX	20–3	SALFORD
1946	WAKEFIELD TRINITY	13–12	WIGAN
1947	BRADFORD NORTHERN	8–4	LEEDS
1948	WIGAN	8–3	BRADFORD NORTHERN
1949	BRADFORD NORTHERN	12–0	HALIFAX
1950	WARRINGTON	19–0	WIDNES
1951	WIGAN	10–0	BARROW
1952	WORKINGTON TOWN	18–10	FEATHERSTONE ROVERS
1953	HUDDERSFIELD	15–10	ST HELENS
1954	WARRINGTON	4–4	HALIFAX
	WARRINGTON	8–4 Replay (Odsal)	HALIFAX
1955	BARROW	21–12	WORKINGTON TOWN
1956	ST HELENS	13–2	HALIFAX
1957	LEEDS	9–7	BARROW
1958	WIGAN	13–9	WORKINGTON TOWN
1959	WIGAN	30–13	HULL

1960	WAKEFIELD TRINITY	38–5	HULL
1961	ST HELENS	12–6	WIGAN
1962	WAKEFIELD TRINITY	12–6	HUDDERSFIELD
1963	WAKEFIELD TRINITY	25–10	WIGAN
1964	WIDNES	13–5	HULL KINGSTON R
1965	WIGAN	20–16	HUNSLET
1966	ST HELENS	21–2	WIGAN
1967	FEATHERSTONE R	17–12	BARROW
1968	LEEDS	11–10	WAKEFIELD TRINITY
1969	CASTLEFORD	11–6	SALFORD
1970	CASTLEFORD	7–2	WIGAN
1971	LEIGH	24–7	LEEDS
1972	ST HELENS	16–13	LEEDS
1973	FEATHERSTONE R	33–14	BRADFORD NORTHERN
1974	WARRINGTON	24–9	FEATHERSTONE R
1975	WIDNES	14–7	WARRINGTON
1976	ST HELENS	20–5	WIDNES
1977	LEEDS	16–7	WIDNES
1978	LEEDS	14–12	ST HELENS
1979	WIDNES	12–3	WAKEFIELD TRINITY
1980	HULL KINGSTON R	10–5	HULL
1981	WIDNES	18–9	HULL KINGSTON R
1982	HULL	14–14	WIDNES
	HULL	19–9 Replay (Elland Rd)	WIDNES
1983	FEATHERSTONE R	14–12	HULL
1984	WIDNES	19–6	WIGAN
1985	WIGAN	28–24	HULL
1986	CASTLEFORD	15–14	HULL KINGSTON R
1987	HALIFAX	19–18	ST HELENS
1988	WIGAN	32–12	HALIFAX
1989	WIGAN	27–0	ST HELENS
1990	WIGAN	36–14	WARRINGTON
1991	WIGAN	13–8	ST HELENS
1992	WIGAN	28–12	CASTLEFORD
1993	WIGAN	20–14	WIDNES
1994	WIGAN	26–16	LEEDS
1995	WIGAN	30–10	LEEDS
1996	ST HELENS	40–32	BRADFORD BULLS
1997	ST HELENS	32–22	BRADFORD BULLS
1998	SHEFFIELD EAGLES	17–8	WIGAN WARRIORS
1999	LEEDS RHINOS	52–16	LONDON BRONCOS

Rugby League — Internationals

INTERNATIONALS

1930	AUSTRALIA	26–10	WALES
1933	AUSTRALIA	51–19	WALES
1963	AUSTRALIA	28–2	GREAT BRITAIN
1973	AUSTRALIA	21–12	GREAT BRITAIN
1990	AUSTRALIA	19–12	GREAT BRITAIN
1993	NEW ZEALAND	0–17	GREAT BRITAIN
1994	AUSTRALIA	4–8	GREAT BRITAIN
1997	AUSTRALIA SUPER LEAGUE	38–14	GREAT BRITAIN

Rugby Union — Internationals

INTERNATIONALS

1992	ENGLAND	26–13	CANADA
1997	NEW ZEALAND	42–7	WALES

FIVE NATIONS

1998	SCOTLAND	13–19	WALES
1998	FRANCE	51–0	WALES
1998	SOUTH AFRICA	28–20	WALES
1999	IRELAND	29–23	WALES
1999	ENGLAND	31–32	WALES

Index

Credits and Acknowledgments

Picture captions for pages 4–25

1923 PC George Scorey controls the crowd on his horse Billy at the first Wembley FA Cup Final between West Ham United and Bolton Wanderers in 1923. Bolton won 2–0 in front of an estimated 200,000 fans.

1924 Her Majesty Queen Mary walks through the grounds of the British Empire Exhibition at Wembley, 1924.

1930 Speedway aces in training. Motorcycle racers Ronnie Moore (right) and Ronnie Mountford prepare for the World Speedway Final at Wembley Stadium in 1962.

1948 Fanny Blankers-Koen of The Netherlands leads the Dutch Women's 400-metre relay team to gold at the 1948 Olympic Games.

1953 Stanley Matthews starts another Blackpool attack in the 1953 FA Cup Final. Thirty-eight-year-old Matthews engineered Blackpool's 4–3 win over Bolton to claim their first major trophy.

1966 English football's finest moment – Bobby Moore holds the Jules Rimet trophy aloft after beating Germany 4–2 in the 1966 World Cup Final.

1977 Scottish fans invade the pitch and destroy the goalposts after beating England 2–1 in the Home International Match at Wembley in 1977.

1985 Richard Skinner announces: It's 12 o'clock in London, 7am in Philadelphia and around the world it's time for Live Aid, sixteen hours of live music in aid of famine relief in Africa. And so began Wembley's most famous rock concert, 1985.

1996 The Dentist's Chair: Paul 'Gazza' Gascoigne celebrates scoring the second goal in England's 2–1 victory over Scotland at Euro '96.

2000 English fans bid farewell during the last ever competitive match at the old Wembley Stadium. England slid to a disappointing 1–0 defeat to its old rival Germany.

2007 The illuminated 'tiara' of steel – a new symbol for Wembley.

Kenneth Powell
I am grateful to Norman Foster, Mouzhan Majidi, Angus Campbell, Alistair Lenczner and Huw Thomas of Foster + Partners and to Rod Sheard and Ben Vickery of HOK Sport for their recollections and reflections on the Wembley project. Nicholas Thompson and Simon Poole of Nathaniel Lichfield & Partners and Bob Heaver provided their own perspectives on the project. Much of the initial research and interviewing for this book was carried out by Tom Weaver, whose editorial skills helped the gestation of my text. As ever, David Jenkins, who conceived the idea of the book, was an inspiring and judicious editor.

Credits
Editing — David Jenkins, Rebecca Roke, Thomas Weaver
Picture research — Sophie Hartley, Thomas Weaver, Kathryn Tollervey
Design — Small (David Hitner / Guy Marshall)
Research — Matthew Foreman, Sophie Hartley, Rebecca Roke, Thomas Weaver
Cutaway drawing — Gregory Gibbon
Proof-reading — Julia Dawson
Index — Hilary Bird
Produced by Firmengruppe APPL

Picture credits
Action Images: 103(1)
Action Images: Roy Beardsworth: 92(2), 122(5); Matthew Childs: 171(7); Andrew Couldridge: 170(2), 171(9); The Football Association/John Marsh Livepic: 170(3); David Jacobs: 122(2,3); MSI: 100(1, 3), 108(2); Tony O'Brien/Livepic: 170(5); Reuters 122(1, 4); John Sibley: 121(4); Sporting Pictures: 114(3); Sporting Pictures, Joe Mann: 114(2); Topham: 12–13; 95; 97(6); WNSL: 170(1)
Action Plus/Glyn Kirk: 71, 72(3)
The Art Archive: 37
Birds Portchmouth Russum: 140–141(old stadium)
Brent Archive: 31(1–3), 51(5), 54(4–6)
Corbis: ©Bettmann: 52(3), 53(8); ©Tim Graham; 173(8); ©Hulton-Deutsch Collection: 8–9, 38(1), 44(3, 4), 45(9), 55, 82; ©Luke MacGregor/Reuters: 173(7); ©Neal Preston: 65(8); ©Andy Rain/epa: 171(8); ©Peter Turnley: 67, 68(3)
Norman Foster: 130, 133, 142, 145
Foster + Partners: 32, 127(1–3), 128, 134(1), 137(1–3), 140–141(new stadium), 143–144, 147
Getty Images: 65(10)
Getty Images: AFP/Carl de Souza: 170(4, 6); AFP/Adrian Dennis: 172(5); Allsport/Shaun Botterill: 73(4, 5), 116(2), 123; Allsport/Clive Brunskill: 117(5); Allsport/Simon Bruty: 72(2), 88(1, 2), 120(2); Allsport/David Cannon: 112–113, 115(6); Allsport/John Gichigi: 91(1); Allsport/Hulton: 80(5); Allsport/Ben Radford: 121(5); Shaun Botterill: 117(3), 167(8); Central Press: 4–5, 6–7, 42(2), 53(7), 96(2), 100(2), 103(2, 4), 105(5); Central Press/Dennis Oulds: 85(4); Georges DeKeerle: 18–19, 63; Express/Robert Stiggins: 105(6); Express/Victor Drees: 108(1); Stu Forster: 20–21; Fox Photos: 56(1), 79(1), 87; Fox Photos/George Freston: 26; Fox Photos/William Vanderson: 79(2), 85(2); Bert Hardy: 54(2); Dave Hogan: 172(2–4); Hulton Archive: 34, 42(3), 51(7), 96(3); Hulton Archive/Central Press: 111; Hulton Archive/Evening Standard: 105(7); Hulton Archive/Fox Photos: 107; Hulton Archive/Dave Hogan: 65(7); Hulton Archive/Dennis Oulds: 99; Hulton Archive/Picture Post: 51(4); Keystone: 45(8), 103(5); Keystone/David Ashdowne: 110; Keystone/Joe Waldorf: 85(3); Keystone/Wesley: 101(4), 109(7); Picture Post/Bert Hardy 54(3); Ben Radford: 88(5); Time & Life Pictures/Brian Seed: 60; Topical Press Agency: 33, 38(5), 41, 45(6), 52(4), 96(1), 97(7); Topical Press Agency/E. Bacon: 45(7); Topical Press Agency/Brooke: 38(2), 45(5); Topical Press Agency/J A Hampton: 54(1); Topical Press Agency/MacGregor: 42(1); Topical Press Agency/Stevens: 38(4); William Vanderson: 85(1); Wesley: 101(6)
The Illustrated London News Picture Library: 44(2)
Mary Evans Picture Library: 56(3);
Mary Evans/Chris Coupland: 51(6),
The National Archives Image Library: 50(3)
Private collection: 43(5–6)
Popperfoto.com: 10–11, 14–15, 16–17, 38(3), 44(1), 49, 50(1, 2), 52(1, 2, 5) 53(6, 9), 56(2, 4–6), 57(7–9), 64(4), 72(1), 73(6–8), 76, 79(3, 4), 80(1–4), 88(3, 4), 91(3), 92(3), 96(4, 5), 97(8), 101(5), 102, 103(3, 6, 7), 104(1–4), 108(3–6), 109(8–12), 114(1, 4, 5), 115(7, 8), 117(4), 118 (1–6), 119, 120(1, 3), 121(6, 7)
Rex Features: 64(1, 3, 5), 91(2), 116(1);
Rex Features: Eugene Adebari: 69(5, 7); Nigel Barklie: 92(1); Martin Beddall: 69(11); Andre Csillag: 69(9); David Fisher: 172(1); Nils Jorgensen: 64(2), 65(9), 68(1, 2, 4); Brian Rasic: 69(8); Richard Young: 69(6)
Topfoto: 59
Topfoto: Star Images: 69(10); UPP: 22–23, 61
H and D White: 64(6)
Nigel Young/Foster + Partners: cover image, 24–25, 134(2–3), 139, 146, 150 (1–8) , 150–151 (1–9), 152 (1–4), 153, 154 (1–3), 155 (4–6), 156–157, 159, 160 (1–3) ,161 (4–7), 162 (1–3), 163(4–6), 164–165, 166 (1–5), 167 (7), 169, 173(6, 7), 174–175